Primary Mathematics
Challenging Word Problems

U.S. Edition

Joseph D. Lee

Primary 6

EPB PAN PACIFIC

Published by EPB Pan Pacific

An imprint of Panpac Education Private Limited
Times Centre
1 New Industrial Road
Singapore 536196

Panpac Education

Email: panpmktg@panpaceducation.com
Website: http://www.panpaceducation.com

EPB Pan Pacific is a trademark of Times Publishing Limited

ISBN 978-981-271-970-6

First published 2004
Reprinted 2006
Reprinted 2007

Distributed in the U.S.A. by SingaporeMath.com Inc

SingaporeMath.com Inc

Printed by Utopia Press Pte Ltd

Printed in Singapore

Preface

Primary Mathematics Challenging Word Problems provides extra practice and challenge in solving word problems. It is written to complement the Primary Mathematics U.S. Edition textbooks and workbooks and follows the same sequence of topics.

The main objective of these books is to help the students improve their problem solving skills. To achieve this, a systematic coverage of most topics from the Primary Mathematics with their relevant exercises has been designed. The language used is simple and clear.

The books incorporate the following features:

Topical Problems — Each book is divided into units containing word problems pertaining to a particular topic.

Review Problems — Each book also includes one or more units of Review Problems that help the students to review and reinforce the skills acquired in the preceding topics.

Answer Key — Each book has an answer key at the end of the book for the student or the instructor to check the answers.

Worked Examples — Each unit of topical problems has three worked examples where the student is guided step by step towards solving the various types of word problems.

Practice Problems — Each unit and each set of review problems contain practice problems where the student can practice solving common word problems based on the topic.

Challenging Problems — The practice problems are followed by challenging word problems which require more thinking skills and creative problem solving strategies.

How to use this book

- Read the worked examples and try to solve them on your own using a separate sheet of paper.

- Compare your solution to the given solution.

- If your answer is correct, congratulate yourself.

- If your solution is different, compare it to the given solution. A problem can have more than one good method of arriving at the same answer.

- If your answer is incorrect, try to understand where you went wrong.

- Then, try to solve the problems in the Practice Problems exercise.

- If you cannot solve one, do not give up. Think about it for a while. Try again later.

- When you have finished, check your answers by referring to the Answer Key.

- If you have an incorrect answer, find out where and why you have gone wrong. Ask for help if you need it.

- Next, try the problems in the Challenging Problems exercise.

- If you cannot solve some of the challenging problems, do not be disheartened or disappointed. They are more challenging than the usual word problems.

- After you have worked on a problem for a while and still cannot solve it, ask for help, and try to understand the solution. Then try to solve it on your own again later.

- The more you practice, the better you will get.

Contents

ALGEBRA

WORKED EXAMPLE 1

Angelica had $250. She bought 8 shirts at $x each.
(a) Express the amount of money she had left in terms of x.
(b) If x = 10, how much money did she have left?

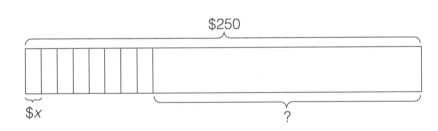

$250

$x

?

(a) Total cost of the 8 shirts = $8 \times x = \$8x$

Amount of money Angelica had left $= \$250 - \$8x$
$= \$(250 - 8x)$

She had **$(250 – 8x)** left.

(b) If x = 10, then

$$250 - 8x = 250 - (8 \times 10)$$
$$= 250 - 80$$
$$= 170$$

She had **$170** left.

Jeffrey had y cookies. He ate 8 cookies and shared the remaining cookies among his 6 cousins equally.
(a) How many cookies did each cousin receive? Express your answer in terms of y.
(b) If $y = 80$, how many cookies did each cousin receive?

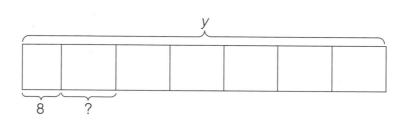

(a) After eating 8 cookies, Jeffrey had $(y - 8)$ cookies left.

$$(y - 8) \div 6 = \frac{y - 8}{6}$$

Each cousin received $\frac{y - 8}{6}$ cookies.

(b) If $y = 80$, then $\frac{y - 8}{6} = \frac{80 - 8}{6}$

$$= \frac{72}{6}$$
$$= 12$$

Each cousin received **12 cookies**.

Andrew has $3z. James has three times as much money as Andrew. Peter has z times as much money as James.
(a) How much money do the three boys have in all? Give your answer in terms of z.
(b) If z = 4, how much money do the three boys have in all?

$3z

Andrew

James

Peter

} ?

(a) Amount of money James has = 3 × 3z
= $9z

Amount of money Peter has = z × 9z
= $9z²

Total amount of money the 3 boys have = 3z + 9z + 9z²
= $(12z + 9z²)

The three boys have **$(12z + 9z²)** in all.

(b) If z = 4, then 12z + 9z² = (12 × 4) + (9 × 4 × 4)
= 48 + 144
= 192

The three boys have **$192** in all.

Answer each of the following questions. Show your work and write your statements clearly.

1. Jane had 100 beads. She gave k beads to each of her 4 friends.
    (a) How many beads did she have left? Express your answer in terms of k.
    (b) If $k = 9$, how many beads did she have left?

2. Henry bought 18 postcards. Mark bought x times as many postcards as Henry.
    (a) How many postcards did they buy altogether? Express your answer in terms of x.
    (b) If $x = 3$, how many postcards did they buy altogether?

3. Calvin had 90 paper-clips. After he bought another m paper-clips, he had twice as many paper-clips as Jack.
    (a) How many paper-clips did Jack have? Express your answer in terms of m.
    (b) If $m = 20$, how many paper-clips did Jack have?

4. Lisa bought 7 books at $a each and a magazine for $14.
   (a) How much money did she spend in all? Express your answer in terms of a.
   (b) If $a = 15$, how much money did she spend in all?

5. Richard bought 8 kg of flour. He gave the cashier $50 and received $p change.
   (a) Find the cost of each kg of flour. Express your answer in terms of p.
   (b) If $p = 18$, find the cost of each kg of flour.

6. David bought 6 pens at $y each and y writing pads at $2 each.
   (a) How much money did he pay altogether? Express your answer in terms of y.
   (b) If $y = 2$, how much money did he pay altogether?

7.   Benjamin has $4z. Vincent has three times as much money as Benjamin. Perry has $8 more than Vincent.
     (a)   How much money does Perry have? Express your answer in terms of z.
     (b)   If z = 14, how much money does Perry have?

8.   Darren paid a deposit of $5q for a refrigerator. He made the rest of the payment in 24 monthly installments. If he paid a total of $23q for the refrigerator,
     (a)   find his monthly installment in terms of q.
     (b)   find his monthly installment if q = 40.

9.   The monthly pay, P in dollars, of a worker is given by P = 1 200 + 5t, where t is the number of hours he has worked overtime in that month.
     (a)   Find his pay in June if he worked 24 hours overtime.
     (b)   Find his pay in July if he worked 35 hours overtime.

10. Lucy had 40a$. She bought 5 books at 3a$ each and 3 plates at 2a$ each.
    (a) How much money did she have left? Express your answer in terms of a.
    (b) If $a = 4$, how much money did she have left?

11. May and Jane have 21b beads altogether. May has 5b more beads than Jane.
    (a) How many beads does May have? Leave your answer in terms of b.
    (b) If $b = 27$, how many beads does May have?

12. Cindy bought 3 erasers for 2c$ and 6 notebooks for 12c$. Each notebook cost more than each eraser.
    (a) How much more did each notebook cost than each eraser? Give your answer in terms of c.
    (b) If $c = \frac{3}{4}$, how much more did each notebook cost than each eraser?

Answer each of the following questions. Show your work and write your statements clearly.

13. Roger had 120 marbles. After he gave n marbles to Ian, $2n$ marbles to Sam and $3n$ marbles to John, Roger had no marbles left.
    (a) Find the value of n.
    (b) How many marbles did Roger give to Sam?

14. Betty has $4s$ beads. Jenny has twice as many beads as Betty. Wendy has 28 fewer beads than Jenny.
    (a) How many beads do the three girls have in all? Express your answer in terms of s.
    (b) If $s = 8$, how many beads do the three girls have in all?

15. Jamie has $3w$ stickers. Joey has w times as many stickers as Jamie. Mick has $2w$ times as many stickers as Jamie.
    (a) How many stickers do the three children have on the average? Express your answer in terms of w.
    (b) If $w = 6$, how many stickers do the three children have on the average?

16. A rectangular piece of cloth is $35x$ cm long and $27x$ cm wide. 4 square pieces of cloth, whose sides are $8x$ cm each, are cut away from its corners.
    (a) Find the perimeter of the remaining piece of cloth. Express your answer in terms of x.
    (b) If $x = 5$, find the perimeter of the remaining piece of cloth.

17. Angela bought some cloth at $2p$ per yard. Using this cloth, she made $3p$ dresses and still had $3p^2$ yd of cloth left. She used $2p$ yd of cloth to make each dress.
    (a) How much money did she pay for all the cloth? Give your answer in terms of p.
    (b) If $p = 2$, how much money did she pay for all the cloth?

18. The floor of a rectangular room measures $24q$ cm by $18q$ cm. It is to be covered with tiles, each measuring $2q$ cm by 12 cm.
    (a) Find the number of tiles needed, giving your answer in terms of q.
    (b) If $q = 16$, find the number of tiles needed.

19. Alvin has three times as much money as Jim. Jim has twice as much money as Paul. If Alvin has $4x,
    (a) how much money do the three boys have altogether? Give your answer in terms of x.
    (b) how much money do the three boys have altogether if x = 12?

20. Jack had $6p. He bought 4 comic books at $\frac{p}{2}$ each and 3 pens at $2 each.
    (a) How much money did he have left? Express your answer in terms of p.
    (b) If p = 5, how much money did he have left?

21. A rectangular container is 6k cm long, 5k cm wide and 2k cm high. It is filled with water to a depth of 7 cm.
    (a) How much more water is needed to completely fill the container? Express your answer in terms of k.
    (b) If k = 18, how much more water is needed to completely fill the container?

RATIO

WORKED EXAMPLE 1

The ratio of the number of Sam's marbles to the number of Winston's marbles was 8 : 3. After Sam gave 45 marbles to Winston, they had the same number of marbles. How many marbles did Sam have at first?

Before

Sam

Winston

8 + 3 = 11 units

After

Sam

Winston

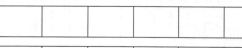

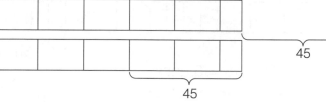

45

45

5 units → 45 + 45 = 90 marbles

1 unit → 90 ÷ 5 = 18 marbles

8 units → 8 × 18 = 144 marbles

Sam had **144** marbles at first.

The number of Joe's stickers and Fred's stickers are in the ratio 5 : 8. The number of Fred's stickers and May's stickers are in the ratio 6 : 5. If Joe has 10 stickers fewer than may, how many stickers does Fred have?

Joe

Fred

Fred

May

Joe

Fred ?

May

10

20 − 15 = 5 units

5 units → 10 stickers
1 unit → 10 ÷ 5
= 2 stickers

24 units → 24 × 2
= 48 stickers

Fred has **48** stickers

Worked Example 3

Tracy had $85 and Agatha had $60. After they donated an equal sum of money to charity, the ratio of Tracy's money to Agatha's money was 12 : 7. How much money did they have left?

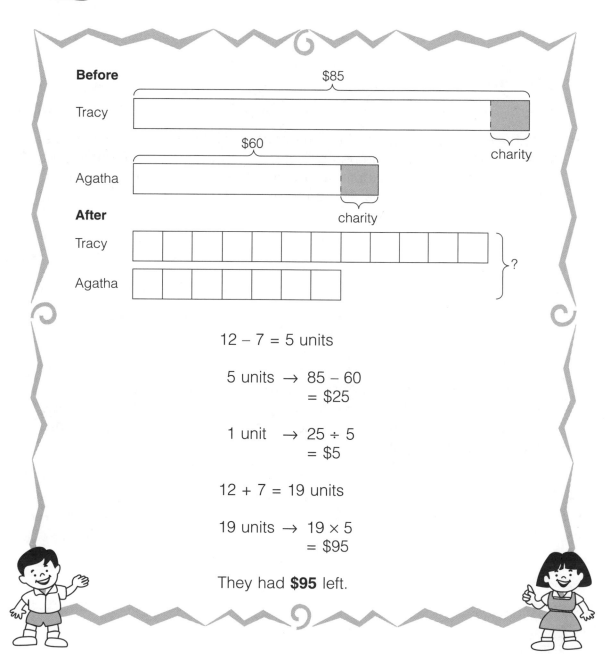

Before

$85

Tracy

$60

Agatha

charity

After

charity

Tracy

Agatha

?

12 − 7 = 5 units

5 units → 85 − 60
= $25

1 unit → 25 ÷ 5
= $5

12 + 7 = 19 units

19 units → 19 × 5
= $95

They had **$95** left.

Answer each of the following questions. Show your work and write your statements clearly.

1. Darren and Mick shared 96 marbles in the ratio 5 : 3. Darren then shared his marbles with Henry in the ratio 11 : 4. How many fewer marbles did Henry get than Mick?

2. At an exhibition, the ratio of the number of adults to the number of children was 8 : 3. The ratio of the number of men to the number of women was 3 : 1. If there were 44 adults and children at the exhibition, how many more children than women were there?

3. The ratio of the number of Ann's picture cards to the number of Wendy's picture cards was 7 : 8. After Wendy gave 8 picture cards to Ann, they each had the same number of picture cards. How many picture cards did they have altogether?

4. Roy and Alan share some stamps in the ratio 4 : 5. $\frac{3}{8}$ of Roy's stamps are Singapore stamps and the rest are Australia stamps. If Roy has 8 more Australia stamps than Singapore stamps, how many stamps does Alan have?

5. Cindy bought 4 shirts and 3 skirts. The amount of money she spent on all the shirts and all the skirts were in the ratio 10 : 9. If she bought each shirt at $15, how much did she pay for each skirt?

6. Alvin's monthly income is $1500. He spends part of this on food, rent and transport in the ratio 1 : 5 : 3. If he spends $200 less on transport than on rent, how much money does he have left after spending on these three items?

7. The ratio of the number of Jimmy's paper-clips to the number of Sam's paper-clips is 3 : 7. 50% of Jimmy's paper-clips and 75% of Sam's paper-clips are red. If Sam has 16 more paper-clips than Jimmy, how many more red paper-clips does Sam have than Jimmy?

8. The ratio of the number of Mary's beads to the number of Jane's beads is 4 : 7. The ratio of the number of Jane's beads to the number of Pauline's beads is 5 : 2. If Mary has 6 more beads than Pauline, how many beads does Jane have?

9. Jack's and Angie's savings are in the ratio 21 : 8. Angie's and Hazel's savings are in the ratio 4 : 9. If the three students have a total savings of $94, how much more savings does Jack have than Hazel?

10. Maria had Spanish storybooks and English storybooks in the ratio 5 : 7. After she bought 34 storybooks, she had three times as many Spanish storybooks and twice as many English storybooks as before. How many storybooks did she have at first?

11. The number of Paul's toy soldiers and toy cars are in the ratio 3 : 4. If he throws away $\frac{1}{3}$ of his toy soldiers and $\frac{1}{2}$ of his toy cars, he will have 24 toy soldiers and toy cars left. How many toy soldiers and toy cars does have have altogether?

12. The ratio of Peter's money to Mark's mone was 7 : 10. After Peter bought 5 comic books at $3.60 each, the ratio of Peter's money to Mark's money was 1 : 4. How much money did Peter and Mark have left?

Challenging Problems

Answers each of the following questions. Show your work and write your statements clearly.

13. Mavis' money and Gina's money were in the ratio 5 : 2. After Mavis spent $1.20 and Gina saved some money so that she now has $3.50, the ratio of Mavis' money to Gina's money was 4 : 5. How much money did Mavis have at first?

14. May and Jane shared some beads in the ratio 2 : 7. After Jane gave $\frac{2}{3}$ of her beads to May, she had 26 fewer beads than May. How many beads were there altogether?

15. The ratio of the number of Roger's marbles to the number of Calvin's marbles was 3 : 8. After Roger bought another 12 marbles and Calvin gave away 28 marbles, they each had the same number of marbles. How many marbles did they have altogether at first?

16. The ratio of the number of men to the number of women at a buffet was 7 : 5. Another 18 men and women joined the buffet and the ratio of the number of men to the number of women became 4 : 3. If there were 54 women at the buffet in the end, how many men joined the buffet?

17. The ratios of the number of chairs to the number of tables in halls A and B are 5 : 2 and 6 : 1 respectively. The total number of chairs and tables in hall B is three times that in hall A. What is the ratio of the number of tables in hall A to the number of chairs in hall B?

18. The ratio of Sally's age to Lucy's age is 8 : 5. 30 years later, this ratio will be 6 : 5. How much older is Sally than Lucy now?

19. A clown had 42 red balloons and 66 blue balloons. After he gave an equal number of red balloons and blue balloons away, the ratio of the number of red balloons to the number of blue balloons he had left was 4 : 7. How many balloons did he give away altogether?

20. George and Alfred had the same number of greeting cards. After George used 6 greeting cards and Alfred used 30 greeting cards, the ratio of the number of George's greeting cards to the number of Alfred's greeting cards was 7 : 5. How many greeting cards did they have left?

21. Three boxes, A, B and C, had 260 ping pong balls. Lisa added some ping pong balls into box A and the number of ping pong balls in box A tripled. She took out half of the ping pong balls in box B and added 40 ping pong balls into box C. The ratio of the number of ping pong balls in boxes A, B and C became 6 : 4 : 5. Find the original ratio of the number of ping pong balls in boxes A, B and C.

PERCENTAGE

WORKED EXAMPLE 1

Eric has 75% as much money as Joshua. Carl has 60% as much money as what Eric and Joshua have altogether. If Eric has $36 less than Carl, how much money does Joshua have?

100%

Joshua

?

75% × 100% = 75%

Eric

60% × (100 + 75)% = 105%

Carl

$36

105% − 75% = 30%

30% → $36

1% → 36 ÷ 3 = $1.20

100% → 100 × 1.20 = $120

Joshua has **$120**.

A man always gives 40% of his monthly income to his wife. When his income increased by 10% between May and June, he gave $120 more to his wife in June than in May. Find his income in June.

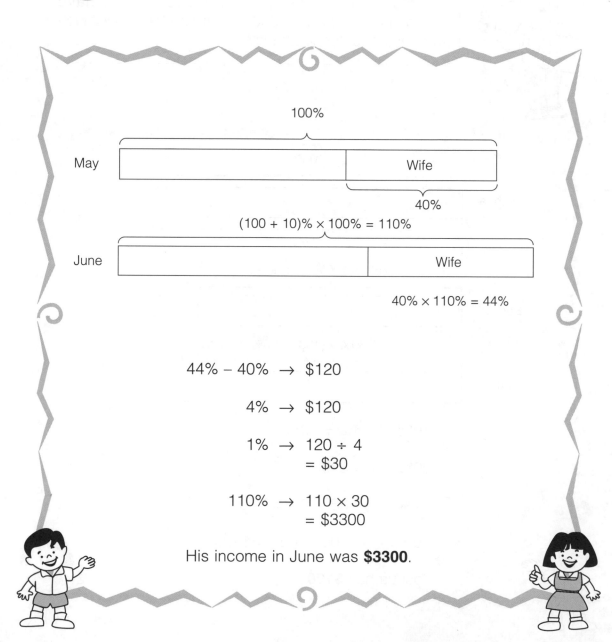

100%

May

Wife

40%

(100 + 10)% × 100% = 110%

June

Wife

40% × 110% = 44%

44% − 40% → $120

4% → $120

1% → 120 ÷ 4
= $30

110% → 110 × 30
= $3300

His income in June was **$3300**.

Bag A had twice as many beads as bag B. After 12% of the beads in bag A and 20% of the beads in bag B were transferred to bag C, the number of beads in bag C increased by 22%. If bag C had 488 beads in the end, how many beads were there in bag A in the end?

Before   100%

Bag C

After $(100 + 22)\% \times 100\% = 122\%$

Bag C

488

$$122\% \rightarrow 488 \text{ beads}$$
$$1\% \rightarrow 488 \div 122 = 4 \text{ beads}$$
$$22\% \rightarrow 22 \times 4 = 88 \text{ beads}$$

Before   200%

Bag A

100%

Bag B

After $12\% \times 200\% = 24\%$

Bag A

$20\% \times 100\% = 20\%$

Bag B

$$24\% + 20\% \rightarrow 88 \text{ beads}$$
$$44\% \rightarrow 88 \text{ beads}$$
$$1\% \rightarrow 88 \div 44 = 2 \text{ beads}$$
$$200\% - 24\% = 176\%$$
$$176\% \rightarrow 176 \times 2 = 352 \text{ beads}$$

There were **352** beads in bag A in the end.

Practice Problems

Answer each of the following questions. Show your work and write your statements clearly.

1. Jasmine's monthly income is $1200. She spends 15% of it on food, 20% of it on rent, $\frac{1}{10}$ of it on transport and 40% of the remainder on others. If she saves the rest of her income, find her yearly savings.

2. Anthony used 14% of his money to buy 7 binders at $4 each. He also used $12\frac{1}{2}$% of his money to buy a paper tray and 21% of his money to buy 3 boxes of pens. How much more did the paper tray cost than each box of pens?

3. A shop owner bought 800 shirts. He bought 15% of them at $9 each, 20% of them at $12 each, $\frac{3}{8}$ of them at $15 each and $\frac{3}{4}$ of the remainder at $10 each. If he paid a total of $440 for the rest of the shirts, how much did he pay for all the shirts?

4. At a sale, Dorothy bought a dress at a discount of 15% for $272 and a watch at a discount of 10% for $2700. How much did she save on the two sale items?

5. 10% of May's beads are red, 35% of them are blue and 50% of the remainder are yellow. If she has 6 more blue beads than yellow beads, how many more yellow beads than red beads does she have?

6. 45% of the spectators at a stadium were men, 30% of them were women, 40% of the remainder were girls and the rest were boys. If there were 120 more boys than girls, how many more men than women were there?

7. After giving 25% of her stickers away, May had 50% as many stickers as Rose. If they had 200 stickers altogether at first, how many stickers did Rose have?

8. Rick has 25% as many stamps as Gabriel. Mark has 70% as many stamps as what Rick and Gabriel have altogether. If Mark has 50 stamps more than Rick, how many stamps do the three boys have altogether?

9. Jimmy has 200 stamps. Mark has 65% as many stamps as Jimmy and Paul has 80% as many stamps as Jimmy. If Jimmy gives 30% of his stamps to Mark and 60% of the remainder to Paul, how many more stamps does Paul have than Mark now?

10. Angela bought a necklace for $2000. When the value of her necklace increased by 20%, she sold it at a discount of 10% off its new value. With this money, she bought a furniture set at a 20% discount. Find the usual selling price of the furniture set.

11. The usual selling price of a car was $104,000. It was later sold at a 10% discount and a 17% profit was made. Find the loss that would have been made if it had been sold at a 30% discount.

12. A shop owner marked the selling price of a washing machine such that he would made a 40% profit. He later sold it at a 20% discount and made a profit of $72. What was the original selling price of the washing machine?

Answer each of the following questions. Show your work and write your statements clearly.

13. Aaron and Johnny shared a sum of money. Aaron received $60. If Aaron had received $8 less, the amount of money Johnny received would have increased by 20%. What percentage of the sum of money did Johnny receive?

14. A salesman always saves 30% of his monthly income. When his income increased by 25% in April, his savings in April increased by $150. What was his income in April?

15. Angela saved $2400 of her salary and spent 24% of her salary on herself. She spent the rest of her salary on her family. If the amount of money she spent on her family was 40% of the total amount of money she spent, find her salary.

16. If a watch is sold at a 15% discount, a profit of $550 will be made. If it is sold at a 40% discount, a loss of $200 will be made. What is the cost price of the watch?

17. A shopkeeper sold an air-conditioner at a discount of $200 and made a 50% profit. He sold another identical air-conditioner at a discount of $900 and made a loss of $100. Find the usual selling price of each air-conditioner.

18. A retailer bought 6 washing machines at the same cost price. He sold 2 of them at a 35% profit, 3 of them at a 20% profit and the last one at a 5% loss. If he received $4350 altogether, how much did he pay for each washing machine?

19. 30% of the members in a youth club were girls and the rest were boys. When 205 members quit the club, the number of boys decreased by 30% and the number of girls became $\frac{1}{3}$ as many as the original number of girls. How many more boys than girls were there left?

20. Box A had three times as many buttons as box B. After 15% of the buttons in box A and 10% of the buttons in box B were transferred to box C, the number of buttons in box C increased by 33%. If box C had 266 buttons in the end, how many buttons were there in box A in the end?

21. Ron and Ben had a total of 700 picture cards. After Ron gave away 40% of his picture cards and Ben gave away 20% of his picture cards, they each had an equal number of picture cards. How many more picture cards did Ron have than Ben at first?

SPEED

WORKED EXAMPLE 1

At 10:10 a.m., Janice set off from town X to town Y at a constant speed of 80 km/h while Christopher set off from town Y to town X at a constant speed of 100 km/h. At 10:55 a.m., they were still 25 km apart. What was the distance between the two towns?

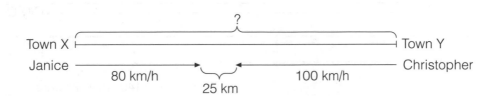

10:10 a.m. to 10:55 a.m. → 45 min = $\frac{3}{4}$ h

At 10:55 a.m.,

distance covered by Janice = $\frac{3}{4} \times 80$
                           = 60 km

distance covered by Christopher = $\frac{3}{4} \times 100$
                                = 75 km

$$60 + 25 + 75 = 160$$

The distance between the two towns was **160 km**.

WORKED EXAMPLE 2

Linda and Jane set off from city P to city Q at uniform speeds at the same time. When Linda reached city Q, Jane was still 140 km away. 2 hours later, Jane also reached city Q. If cities P and Q were 630 km apart, at what speed was Linda travelling?

```
                          630 km
City P •────────────────────────────────────• City Q

Linda  ─────────────────────────────────────▶

Jane   ──────────────────────────────▶
                                       └──────┘
                                    140 km in 2 hours
```

Jane's speed = 140 ÷ 2
              = 70 km/h

Time Jane took to reach city Q = 630 ÷ 70
                               = 9 hours

Time Linda took to reach city Q = 9 − 2
                                = 7 hours

Linda's speed = 630 ÷ 7
              = 90 km/h

Linda was travelling at a speed of **90 km/h**.

Towns A and B were 625 km apart. At 5:30 p.m., Andrew drove from town A to town B at a constant speed of 100 km/h. 15 minutes later, Jack drove from town B to town A at a constant speed of 80 km/h. At what time did they pass each other on the road?

625 km

Town A •————————————————————• Town B

Andrew ——————→
100 km/h

←————— Jack
80 km/h

Distance Andrew had covered before Jack started

his journey = $\frac{15}{60}$ × 100

= 25 km

Distance apart between Andrew and Jack when Jack started his journey = 625 − 25

= 600 km

Total distance Andrew and Jack travelled per hour
= 100 + 80
= 180 km

Time Andrew and Jack took to pass each other
= 600 ÷ 180

= $3\frac{1}{3}$ hours

Time Andrew and Jack passed each other

→ 5:30 p.m. + 15 minutes + $3\frac{1}{3}$ hours

→ 5:45 p.m. + 3 hours 20 minutes

→ 9:05 p.m.

They passed each other on the road at **9:05 p.m.**

Answer each of the following questions. Show your work and write your statements clearly.

1. Shawn took 9 hours to travel 880 km. For the first 180 km, he took 2 hours. What was his average speed for the rest of the journey?

2. Lisa drove at a uniform speed of 76 km/h for 30 minutes and then at a uniform speed of 80 km/h for 45 minutes. Find her average speed for the whole journey.

3. Bobby took 6 hours to drive from town A to town B. He drove at an average speed of 65 km/h for the first 3 hours and then at an average speed of 72 km/h for the rest of the journey. Find the distance between towns A and B.

4. A man set off from city X to city Y at 2:20 p.m. For the first 125 miles, he travelled at an average speed of 50 mi/h. For the remaining 140 miles, he travelled at an average speed of 70 mi/h. At what time did he reach his destination?

5. Peter drove at an average speed of 120 km/h for $3\frac{1}{2}$ hours. If he had increased his speed by 20 km/h, how much time would he have saved?

6. Ricky took 5 hours to travel from town P to town Q at an average speed of 60 mi/h. Sam took 1 hour more than Ricky to complete the same journey. Find Sam's average speed for the whole journey.

7. John and Paul set off from town X to town Y, at constant speeds of 90 km/h and 60 km/h respectively, at the same time. How far apart were they after $2\frac{1}{2}$ hours?

8. A motorcyclist left town X to town Y at a constant speed of 96 km/h and then continued from town Y to town Z at a constant speed of 108 km/h. If he took 1 h 12 min to travel from town X to town Y and 1 h 20 min to travel from town Y to town Z, find the total distance he covered.

9. Town A and town B were 150 km apart. Richard drove from town A to town B at an average speed of 60 km/h. How much earlier would he have arrived at town B if he had travelled at an average speed of 80 km/h instead?

10. A car started from town A at a constant speed of 80 km/h towards town B. A truck started from town B at a constant speed of 55 km/h towards town A. If both the car and truck started their journeys at 6:45 p.m. and passed each other at 9:05 p.m., find the distance between town A and town B.

11. A motorcycle and a car were 400 km apart. They started travelling towards each other at 4:00 p.m. at uniform speeds. The motorcycle was travelling at a uniform speed of 100 km/h and it passed the car at 6:30 p.m. Find the speed of the car.

12. At 3:15 p.m., Marcus set off from town A to town B at a constant speed of 72 km/h while Jason set off from town B to town A at a constant speed of 96 km/h. At 4:30 p.m., they had passed each other and were 24 km apart. Find the distance between towns A and B.

Answer each of the following questions. Show your work and write your statements clearly.

13. Janet and Cindy travelled from town M to town N at uniform speeds of 95 km/h and 104 km/h respectively, at the same time. Some time later, they were 15 km apart. How long had they been travelling?

14. Edwin and Winston set off town X to town Y at uniform speeds at the same time. When Edwin reached town Y, Winston was still 210 km away. 3 hours later, Winston also reached town Y. If the two towns were 560 km apart, at what speed was Edwin travelling?

15. Henry and Tom started driving from the same place but in opposite directions along a straight road. 4 hours later, they were 680 km apart. If Henry was driving at an average speed of 65 km/h, at what average speed was Tom travelling?

16. Andy travelled from town P to town Q at an average speed of 80 km/h. One hour later, Mike also travelled from town P to town Q at an average speed of 100 km/h. If Mike reached town Q $4\frac{1}{2}$ hours later, how far away was Andy from town Q then?

17. Towns M and N were 410 km apart. At 9:15 a.m., Jeffrey set off from town M for town N at an average speed of 80 km/h. 45 minutes later, Marcus set off from town N for town M at an average speed of 120 km/h. At what time did they pass each other?

18. At 1:05 p.m., a van started driving along a straight expressway at a constant speed of 60 km/h. At 1:35 p.m., a car moved off from the same place as the van at a constant speed. After travelling for 210 km, the car caught up with the van. If the van and the car continued travelling at their constant speeds, how far apart would they be at 5:50 p.m.?

19. At 3:40 p.m., a truck left city A for city B at a uniform speed of 51 mi/h. At 4:20 p.m., a minibus also left city A for city B and travelled at a uniform speed of 68 mi/h.
    (a) At what time did the minibus overtake the truck?
    (b) At what time after that would the two vehicles be 51 km apart?

20. Town X and town Y were 270 km apart. A car started from town X towards town Y at a uniform speed of 60 km/h while a motorcycle started from town Y to town X at a uniform speed of 90 km/h. Both the car and the motorcycle started their journeys at 5:15 a.m.
    (a) At what time did they pass each other?
    (b) How far away was the car from town Y when it passed the motorcycle?

21. Town A and town B were 150 km apart. A truck started from town A towards town B at 3:40 p.m. A car also started from town A towards town B half an hour later. The car overtook the truck at 5:40 p.m. when both were 30 km away from town B. If both the car and truck were travelling at constant speeds,
    (a) find the speed of the car.
    (b) how much longer does it take the truck to reach town B than the car?

TOPICAL PROBLEMS 5

FRACTIONS

WORKED EXAMPLE 1

Ann gave $\frac{1}{4}$ of her beads to Joey, $\frac{3}{16}$ of them to May and $\frac{1}{5}$ of the rest to Rose. If Ann had 36 beads left, how many beads did she have at first?

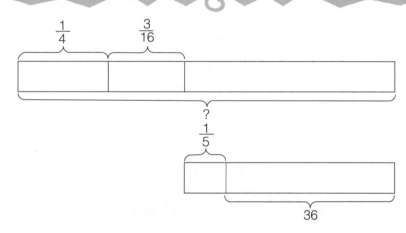

After giving part of her beads to Joey and May, fraction of Ann's beads left = $1 - \frac{1}{4} - \frac{3}{16} = \frac{16}{16} - \frac{4}{16} - \frac{3}{16} = \frac{9}{16}$

After giving part of her beads to Rose, fraction of Ann's beads left $= \left(1 - \frac{1}{5}\right) \times \frac{9}{16} = \frac{4}{5} \times \frac{9}{16} = \frac{9}{20}$

Number of beads Ann had at first = $36 \div \frac{9}{20}$

$= 36 \times \frac{20}{9} = 80$

She had **80** beads at first.

Henry has $\frac{3}{4}$ as many paper-clips as Joyce. Joyce has $\frac{4}{5}$ as many paper-clips as Claire. If the three girls have 96 paper-clips altogether, how many fewer paper-clips does Henry have than Claire?

Claire					
Joyce					
Henry					

96

?

5 + 4 + 3 = 12 units

12 units → 96 paper-clips

1 unit → 96 ÷ 12
        = 8 paper-clips

5 − 3 = 2 units

2 units → 2 × 8
        = 16 paper-clips

Henry has **16** fewer paper-clips than Claire.

John and Rick had 900 stamps altogether. After John used $\frac{2}{7}$ of his stamps and Rick used 180 of his stamps, they had the same number of stamps left. How many stamps did they have left?

Before

John

Rick

} 900

180

Fraction of John's stamps left = $1 - \frac{2}{7} = \frac{5}{7}$

After

John

Rick

?

7 + 5 = 12 units

12 units → 900 − 180 = 720 stamps

1 unit → 720 ÷ 12 = 60 stamps

5 + 5 = 10 units

10 units → 10 × 60
= 600 stamps

They had **600** stamps left.

Practice Problems

Answer each of the following questions. Show your work and write your statements clearly.

1. There are 60 beads in a box. $\frac{3}{10}$ of them are green, $\frac{1}{6}$ of them are blue and $\frac{2}{15}$ of them are red. If the remaining beads are yellow, how many yellow beads are there?

2. Blue pens were sold at 3 for $1, red pens at 4 for $1.20 and black pens at 5 for $2. Cameron bought 5 dozen pens. If $\frac{3}{10}$ of the pens which he bought were blue, $\frac{1}{5}$ of them were red and the rest were black, how much did he pay for all the pens?

3. Macy bought 30 fruits. $\frac{2}{5}$ of them were apples, $\frac{1}{3}$ of them were oranges and $\frac{3}{4}$ of the remainder were pears. If the rest were lemons, how many more pears than lemons did she buy?

4. Jimmy read $\frac{2}{15}$ of a book on Monday, $\frac{1}{3}$ of it on Tuesday, $\frac{2}{9}$ of it on Wednesday and $\frac{3}{4}$ of the remainder on Thursday. If he still had 14 pages left to read on Friday, how many pages were there in the book?

5. Kevin spent $\frac{4}{25}$ of his money on a magazine, $\frac{3}{10}$ of it on a book $\frac{2}{3}$ of the remainder on a dictionary. If he spent $3 more on the dictionary than on the book, how much money did he have at first?

6. Joe, Peter, Mike and Cindy shared some paper-clips. Joe received $\frac{1}{10}$ of the paper-clips, Peter received $\frac{3}{8}$ of them and Mike received $\frac{5}{9}$ of the rest. Cindy received the remaining paper-clips. If Mike received 10 paper-clips fewer than Peter, how many paper-clips did Cindy receive?

7. Wendy saves 30% of her income each month. $\frac{3}{8}$ of her expenditure is spent on cosmetics, $\frac{1}{6}$ of it is spent on transport and $\frac{2}{5}$ of the remainder is spent on food. If she spends $469 on cosmetics and food altogether, how much does she save each month?

8. Mabel has $\frac{5}{8}$ as many stickers as Claire. Claire has $\frac{5}{6}$ as many stickers as Sarah. If the 3 girls have 226 stickers altogether, how many more stickers does Sarah have than Mabel?

9. Mike has $\frac{2}{3}$ as much money as Peter. Peter has $\frac{5}{6}$ as much money as Irene. After Irene bought 3 notebooks at $2.40 each, she had $8.80 more than Mike. How much money did Peter have?

10. David bought $\frac{4}{5}$ kg of vegetables, $\frac{3}{4}$ kg of prawns and $\frac{1}{2}$ kg of meat for $13.20 altogether. He bought the prawns at $10 per kg. If he had not bought the meat but another $\frac{1}{10}$ kg of vegetables instead, he would have spent $2.10 less. How much did he pay for each kg of meat?

11. A man bought 3 sacks of flour at $16 per sack. Each sack of flour weighed 30 kg. He repacked the flour into bags of $\frac{3}{5}$ kg and bags of $1\frac{1}{2}$ kg. There were five times as many $\frac{3}{5}$ kg bags as $1\frac{1}{2}$ kg bags. If he sold each $\frac{3}{5}$ kg bag at $0.50 and each $1\frac{1}{2}$ kg bag at $1.20, how much profit did he make in all?

12. In a class of 40 students, $\frac{3}{8}$ of them play only basketball, $\frac{2}{5}$ play only soccer and $\frac{3}{20}$ play only volleyball. If $\frac{3}{5}$ of those who play basketball and $\frac{1}{4}$ of those who play soccer now also play volleyball, how many students play volleyball altogether?

Answer each of the following questions. Show your work and write your statements clearly.

13. $\frac{2}{3}$ of Amy's stamps is equal to $\frac{2}{5}$ of Betty's stamps. If they have 240 stamps altogether, how many more stamps does Betty have than Amy?

14. Mike and David had 200 paper-clips altogether. After Mike used $\frac{2}{9}$ of his paper-clips and David used 40 of his paper-clips, they had the same number of paper-clips left. How many more paper-clips did David have than Mike at first?

15. Gabriel had $\frac{5}{6}$ as many marbles as James. After James bought 15 more marbles, Gabriel had $\frac{2}{3}$ as many marbles as James. How many marbles did Gabriel have?

16. Mandy had $\frac{5}{8}$ as many beads as Lucy. After Lucy gave $\frac{1}{4}$ of her beads to Mandy, Mandy had 10 beads more than Lucy. How many beads did Mandy have at first?

17. After Mark gave 20 cards to Irene, he had $\frac{1}{3}$ as many cards as Cindy and $\frac{3}{10}$ as many cards as Irene. If the three students had 110 cards altogether, how many fewer cards did Irene have than Mark at first?

18. Jasmine solved an equal number of work problems each day. After 5 days, she had $\frac{7}{12}$ of the word problems left to solve. After another 2 days, she had 25 word problems left to solve. How many word problems did she have to solve at first?

19. Gabriel had three times as many U.S. stamps as Canadian stamps. After he gave $\frac{3}{10}$ of his U.S. stamps and $\frac{2}{5}$ of his Canadian stamps away, Gabriel had 90 more U.S. stamps than Canadian stamps left. How many stamps did he have left?

20. $\frac{1}{2}$ lb of fish costs twice as much as $\frac{4}{5}$ lb of vegetables. If $\frac{7}{10}$ lb of fish and $\frac{1}{2}$ lb of vegetables cost \$13.70 altogether, how much more does each lb of fish cost than each lb of vegetables?

21. Roland had five times as many postcards as Patrick. After Roland gave $\frac{1}{4}$ of his postcards to Patrick, Patrick gave $\frac{1}{6}$ of his postcards to Roland. If Roland had 90 more postcards than Patrick in the end, how many postcards did Roland have at first?

CIRCLES

The figure shows a square ABCD that is 14 cm long. ABQD and CDPB are quadrants. Find the shaded area. (Take π = 3.14)

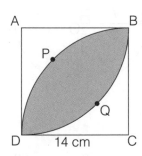

Area of quadrant ABQD = Area of quadrant CDPB

$$= \frac{1}{4} \times 3.14 \times 14 \times 14$$

$$= 153.86 \text{ cm}^2$$

Area of square ABCD = 14 × 14

$$= 196 \text{ cm}^2$$

Shaded area = 153.86 + 153.86 − 196

$$= 111.72 \text{ cm}^2$$

The shaded area is **111.72 cm²**.

WORKED EXAMPLE 2

Find the perimeter of the figure shown.

$\left(\text{Take } \pi = \frac{22}{7} \right)$

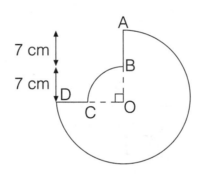

Length of arc AD = $\frac{3}{4} \times 2 \times \frac{22}{7} \times 14$

= 66 cm

Length of arc BC = $\frac{1}{4} \times 2 \times \frac{22}{7} \times 7$

= 11 cm

Perimeter of the figure = 66 + 11 + 7 + 7

= 91 cm

The perimeter of the figure is **91 cm**.

WORKED EXAMPLE 3

What is the area of the figure shown?
(Take π = 3.14)

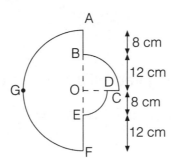

Area of semi-circle AGF $= \frac{1}{2} \times 3.14 \times 20 \times 20$

$\qquad\qquad\qquad\qquad\quad = 628 \text{ cm}^2$

Area of quadrant BCO $= \frac{1}{4} \times 3.14 \times 12 \times 12$

$\qquad\qquad\qquad\qquad = 113.04 \text{ cm}^2$

Area of quadrant DEO $= \frac{1}{4} \times 3.14 \times 8 \times 8$

$\qquad\qquad\qquad\qquad = 50.24 \text{ cm}^2$

Area of the figure = 628 + 113.04 + 50.24

$\qquad\qquad\qquad\quad = 791.28 \text{ cm}^2$

The area of the figure is **791.28 cm²**.

Answer each of the following questions. Show your work and write your statements clearly.

1. In the figure shown, AB = BC = CD = DE = 14 cm. Find the perimeter of the figure. $\left(\text{Take } \pi = \frac{22}{7}\right)$

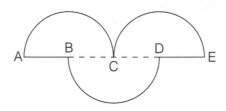

2. The figure shows a running track. If Jim runs around it six times, what is the total distance he will cover? $\left(\text{Take } \pi = \frac{22}{7}\right)$

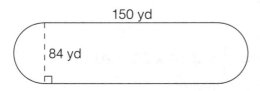

150 yd

84 yd

3. In the figure shown, the area of the square is 169 cm². Find the perimeter of the figure. (Take π = 3.14)

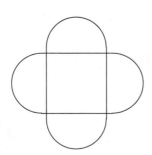

4. The figure shown is made up of a big semi-circle and two smaller semi-circles. O is the center of the big semi-circle and its radius is 20 cm. Find the area of the figure. (Take π = 3.14)

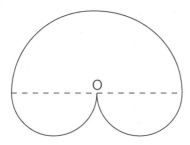

5. In the figure shown, OP = PQ = 16 cm. What is the area of the figure? (Take π = 3.14)

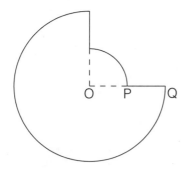

6. In the figure shown, the area where the two circles intersect is 76.5 cm^2. Find the area of the shaded parts. (Take π = 3.14)

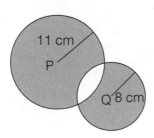

7. The figure shows two circles. The inner circle has a radius of 8 cm and its circumference is 5 cm away from the circumference of the outer circle. Find the shaded area. (Take π = 3.14)

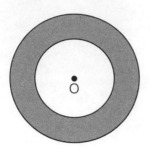

8. In the figure shown, find the perimeter. $\left(\text{Take } \pi = \dfrac{22}{7}\right)$

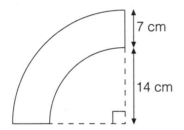

7 cm

14 cm

9. The figure shows two of the lanes at a running track that are 3 m apart. Mary and Jim ran around the track three times, with Mary taking the inner land and Jim taking the outer lane. How much further did Jim cover than Mary? (Take π = 3.14)

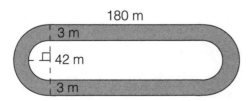

180 m

3 m

42 m

3 m

10. The figure shown is made up of an equilateral triangle and a semi-circle. If the perimeter of the triangle is 27 cm, find the perimeter of the figure. (Take π = 3.14)

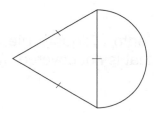

11. In the figure shown, find the area of the rectangle left when the triangle and the quadrant are cut away. (Take π = 3.14)

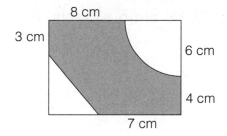

3 cm
8 cm
6 cm
4 cm
7 cm

12. In the figure shown, XY = YZ = 28 cm. Find the area and perimeter of the figure. $\left(\text{Take } \pi = \dfrac{22}{7}\right)$

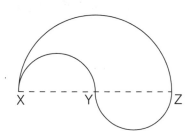

Answer each of the following questions. Show your work and write your statements clearly.

13. Ann pasted a circular piece of paper disc onto a square piece of cardboard. What is the area of the cardboard that is not covered by the disc? (Take $\pi = 3.14$)

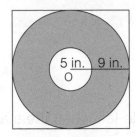

14. In the figure shown, both ABYD and CDXB are quadrants. Find the shaded area. $\left(\text{Take } \pi = \dfrac{22}{7}\right)$

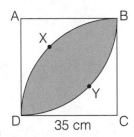

15. In the figure shown, the square has a length of 10 cm and each semi-circle has a diameter of 5 cm. Find the area of the shaded figure. (Take $\pi = 3.14$)

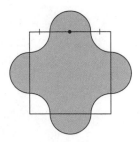

16. In the figure shown, two quadrants of the same radius are put on top of each other such that a square 21 cm long is formed. Find the shaded area. $\left(\text{Take } \pi = \frac{22}{7}\right)$

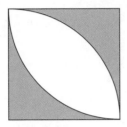

17. In the figure shown, what is the shaded area? $\left(\text{Take } \pi = \frac{22}{7}\right)$

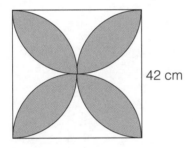

42 cm

18. The figure shows parts of a circle inscribed within a right-angled triangle. What is the area of the unshaded part? (Take $\pi = 3.14$)

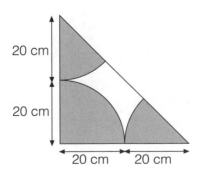

20 cm

20 cm

20 cm   20 cm

19. Find the area of the figure shown. (Take π = 3.14)

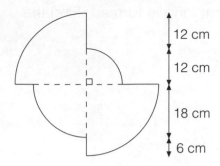

12 cm

12 cm

18 cm

6 cm

20. Find the perimeter of the figure shown. (Take π = 3.14)

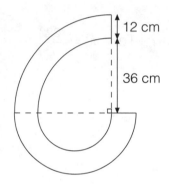

12 cm

36 cm

21. In the figure shown, OP = 42 cm. Find the area of the figure.
$\left(\text{Take } \pi = \dfrac{22}{7}\right)$

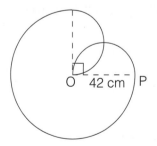

O   42 cm   P

VOLUME

WORKED EXAMPLE 1

A rectangular tank, 16 m long, 9 m wide and 8 m high, is $\frac{1}{3}$ filled with water. Water is pumped in at a rate of 2 m³ per minute through a water pipe, and pumped out at a rate of 0.5 m³ per minute through another water pipe. Find the new water level in the tank 20 minutes later.

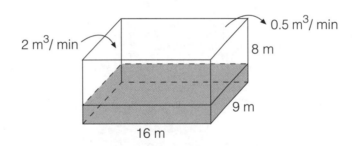

Initial water level in the tank = $\frac{1}{3} \times 8 = 2\frac{2}{3}$ m

Net increase in the volume of water per minute = 2 − 0.5
$$= 1.5 \text{ m}^3$$

Total increase in the volume of water 20 minutes later = 20 × 1.5
$$= 30 \text{ m}^3$$

Increase in the water level 20 minutes later = 30 ÷ (16 × 9)
$$= \frac{5}{24} \text{ m}$$

New water level in the tank 20 minutes later = $2\frac{2}{3} + \frac{5}{24}$
$$= 2\frac{7}{8} \text{ m}$$

The new water level in the tank 20 minutes later is **$2\frac{7}{8}$ m**.

WORKED EXAMPLE 2

In the figure shown, the container has a flat base and is filled with water to a depth of 16 cm. Find the volume of the water in the container.

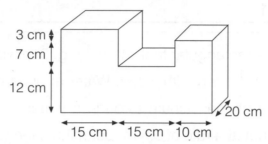

3 cm
7 cm
12 cm
15 cm   15 cm   10 cm
20 cm

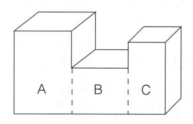

A   B   C

Volume of the water in A = 15 × 20 × 16
= 4800 cm³

Volume of the water in B = 15 × 20 × 12
= 3600 cm³

Volume of the water in C = 10 × 20 × 16
= 3200 cm³

Total volume of the water in the container
= 4800 + 3600 + 3200
= 11,600 cm³

The volume of the water in the container is **11,600 cm³**.

The figure shows three rectangular containers, A, B and C. Container A is first filled with water to a depth of 20 cm. The water is then poured into B, with the remaining water poured into C. Find the depth of the water in C.

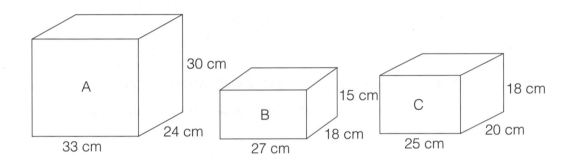

Volume of the water in container A = 33 × 24 × 20
= 15,840 cm^3

Volume of the water poured into = 27 × 18 × 15
container B = 7290 cm^3

Volume of the water poured into = 15,840 − 7290
container C = 8550 cm^3

Depth of the water in container C = 8550 ÷ (25 × 20)
= 17.1 cm

The depth of the water in C is **17.1 cm**.

Practice Problems

Answer each of the following questions. Show your work and write your statements clearly.

1. A rectangular container, 60 cm long, 35 cm wide and 10 cm high, is half filled with water. If water is leaking at a rate of 350 cm³ per minute, how long will it take before the container becomes empty?

2. A rectangular container, when $\frac{2}{5}$ filled with water, contains 40,320 cm³ of water. If it is 84 cm long and 50 cm wide, what is its height?

3. A container, when filled with some water and 4 blocks of metal, has a volume of 1 liter. The volume of the water in the container is 832 cm³. If each block of metal is 7 cm long and 4 cm wide, find its height.
    (1 liter = 1000 cm³)

4. The volume of a rectangular block of wood is 4800 cm³. Its length and width are 32 cm and 15 cm respectively. If 7 cm of it is floating below the water surface in a tank, how much of it is floating above the water surface?

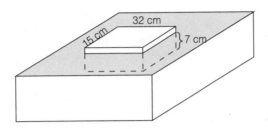

5. In a rectangular container completely filled with water and oil, there are 6480 cm³ of water more than oil. If the container is 48 cm long, 27 cm wide and 18 cm high, find the depth of the water in the container.

6. The length and width of a rectangular container are 40 cm and 25 cm respectively. It is filled with sand and clay in the ratio 2 : 3. If the depth of the sand in the container is 6 cm, how much more clay than sand is there?

7. A rectangular container is $\frac{3}{4}$ filled with oil. The length, width and height of the container are in the ratio 7 : 5 : 3. If its length is 20 cm longer than its height, how much more oil can the container contain?

8. A blacksmith has a rectangular block of metal 32 cm long, 25 cm wide and 15 cm high. He cut a cubical block of metal with a base area of 25 cm² from the side of the metal block. What is the volume of the metal block left?

9. A rectangular tank, 72 cm long, 45 cm wide and 40 cm high, is filled with water to a depth of 17.9 cm. When two identical pieces of metal are added into the tank, the water level rises to 18.1 cm. Find the volume of each piece of metal.

10. A rectangular block of metal 18 cm long, 8.1 cm wide and 5 cm high is melted and recast into a cube. Find the length of each side of the cube.

11. A rectangular container, 25 cm long, 18 cm wide, and 10 cm high, contains 4 *l* 320 ml of water. Another rectangular container, 10 cm long, 6 cm wide and 4 cm high is completely filled with water. If water from the second container is poured into the first container, how much water will overflow?

12. Water is poured into a rectangular container, 20 cm long, 14 cm wide and 9 cm high, until it is $\frac{5}{6}$ full. All this water is then poured into an empty container, 35 cm long, 30 cm wide and 15 cm high. What is the depth of the water in the second container?

Answer each of the following questions. Show your work and write your statements clearly.

13. The interior dimensions of a rectangular box are 54 cm, 30 cm and 12 cm. A man packs as many 4-cm cubes as possible into the box. What volume of the box will not be occupied?

14. An empty rectangular container is 60% as wide as it is long and 50% as high as it is wide. There are a 10-cm cube and an 8-cm cube in it. If the container is 24 cm wide, how much water can be poured into it before it overflows?

15. A rectangular tank, 36 m long, 10 m wide and 5 m high, is at first half filled with water. Water is then pumped in at a rate of 4 m^3 per minute through a water pipe. If water also starts to leak at a rate of 1.5 m^3 per minute, what will be the new water level in the tank $\frac{3}{5}$ hour later?

16. The figure shows a container that is to be completely filled with water. How much water is needed?

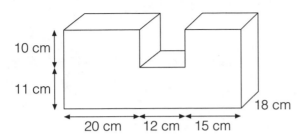

17. In the figure shown, water is filled to a depth of 10 cm. Find the volume of the water in the container.

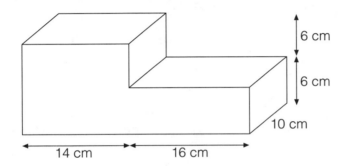

18. An empty rectangular pool, 50 m long, 20 m wide and 3 m deep, is filled with water by two water pipes. One pipe pumps in water at a rate of 2 m³ per minute and the other pipe pumps in water at a rate of 3 m³ per minute. How many hours will it take for both pipes to completely fill the pool with water?

19. The container shown is standing on its base. If water is now poured into it to a depth of 12 cm, how much water will there be?

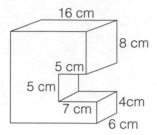

20. In the figure shown, containers A and B each has an opening which, when released, will allow water to flow out if the water level is higher than the opening. Container A is first completely filled with water. Then the openings of both containers A and B are opened. What will be the final water level in container C?

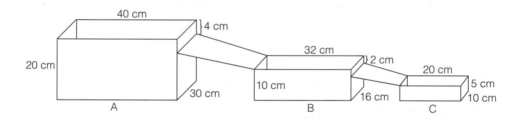

21. A rectangular metal container has external dimensions, 42 cm, 35 cm and 20 cm, and internal dimensions, 36 cm, 27 cm and 15 cm. If each cm³ of water weighs 1 g and each cm³ of metal weighs 2 g, find the total weight of the container when it is fully filled with water.

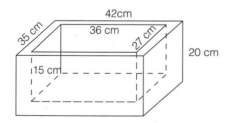

TOPICAL PROBLEMS 8

TRIANGLES AND 4-SIDED FIGURES

In the figure shown, ABCD is a parallelogram, AB // DC // EF and AD // BF. Find ∠x.

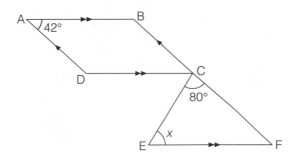

∠a = 180° − 42° (Each pair of angles between two parallel
   = 138°   sides add up to 180°.)

∠b = 180° − 138° (Each pair of
   = 42°   angles
                  between two
                  parallel sides
                  add up to 180°.)

∠x = 180° − 80° − 42° (The sum of the
   = 58°   angles of a triangle is 180°.)

∠x = **58°**

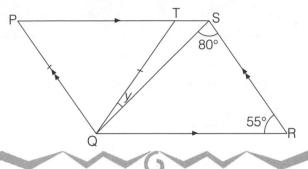

In the figure, not drawn to scale, PQRS is a parallelogram and PQT is an isosceles triangle. Find ∠y.

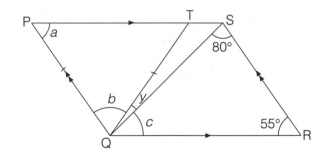

∠a = 55° (The opposite angles of a parallelogram are equal.)

∠b = 180° − (2 × 55°)
   = 70° (The angles opposite the equal sides of an
         isosceles triangle are equal.)

∠c = 180° − 80° − 55° (The sum of the angles of a
   = 45°   triangle is 180°.)

∠b + ∠y + ∠c = 180° − 55° (Each pair of angles between two
                         parallel sides add up to 180°.)

70° + ∠y + 45° = 125°
    ∠y + 115° = 125°
        ∠y = 125° − 115°
           = 10°

∠y = **10°**

In the figure shown, KLM is an isosceles triangle. Find ∠z.

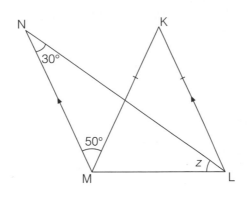

$\angle a = 180° - 50°$ (Each pair of
$\quad = 130°$ angles
                between two
                parallel sides
                add up to 180°.)

$\angle KLM = 130° \div 2$ (The angles
$\qquad\quad = 65°$ opposite the equal
                  sides of an
                  isosceles triangle are
                  equal; the exterior
angle of a triangle is equal to the sum of
the interior opposite angles.)

$\angle b = 180° - 30° - 50°$ (The sum of the angles of a triangle is
$\quad = 100°$ 180°.)
$\angle c = 100°$ (Vertically opposite angles are equal.)
$\angle d = 130° - 100°$ (The exterior angle of a triangle is equal to
$\quad = 30°$ the sum of the interior opposite angles.)
$\angle z = 65° - 30°$
$\quad = 35°$

$$\angle z = \mathbf{35°}$$

Answer each of the following questions. Show your work and write your statements clearly.

1. In the figure shown, ABC is an equilateral triangle. Find ∠a.

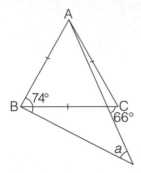

2. In the figure shown, DEF is an isosceles triangle and FG // ED. Find ∠b.

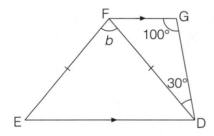

3. In the figure shown, KLM and KNM are isosceles triangles. Find ∠c.

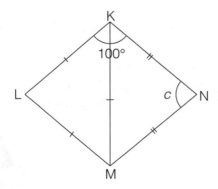

4. In the figure shown, PQ = PR = RS. Find ∠d.

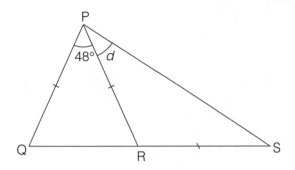

5. In the figure shown, ABCD is a rectangle and DE = FA. Find ∠e.

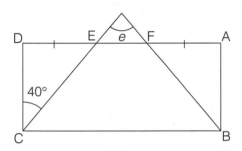

6. In the figure shown, WX = XY and YZ = ZW. Find ∠f and ∠g.

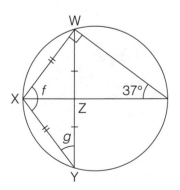

7. In the figure, not drawn to scale, AB // CD and EC // FG. Find ∠h.

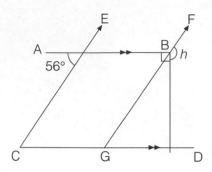

8. In the figure, not drawn to scale PQ // LN and KL // MN. Find ∠k.

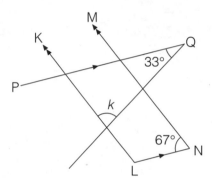

9. In the figure, not drawn to scale, PQR is an isosceles triangle and PRST is a parallelogram. Find ∠m.

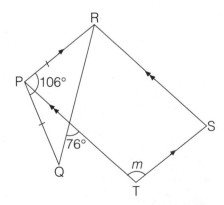

10. In the figure, not drawn to scale, WXYZ is a square. Find ∠n.

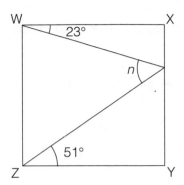

11. In the figure, not drawn to scale, ABCD and ABEF are parallelograms. Find ∠p.

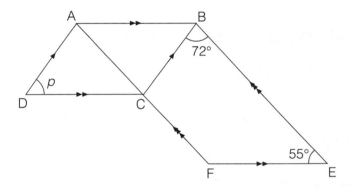

12. In the figure, not drawn to scale, KLMN is a parallelogram and O is the center of the circle. Find ∠q and ∠r.

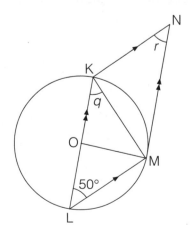

Challenging Problems

Answer each of the following questions. Show your work and write your statements clearly.

13. In the figure shown, O is the center of the semi-circle. Find ∠s.

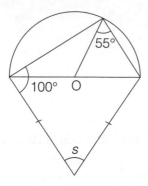

14. In the figure shown, ABCD is a parallelogram. Find ∠t.

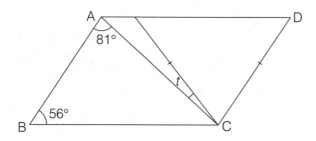

15. In the figure shown, EFG and EHI are isosceles triangles. Find ∠v and ∠w.

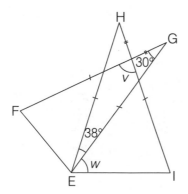

16. In the figure shown, JKL is an isosceles triangle. Find ∠x and ∠y.

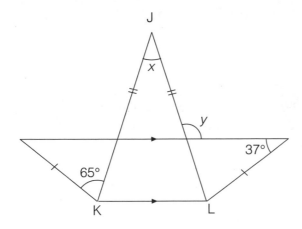

17. In the figure shown, MN // OP // QR and ST // UR // MV. Find ∠x and ∠y.

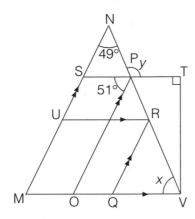

18. In the figure shown, P and Q are the centers of the respective circles. Find ∠a and ∠b.

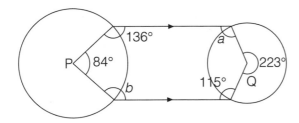

19. In the figure, not drawn to scale, XYZ is an isosceles triangle. Find ∠c.

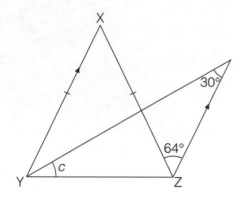

20. In the figure, not drawn to scale, ABCD is a rectangle. Find ∠d.

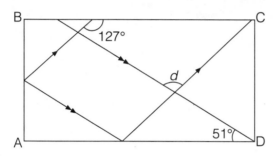

21. The figure shows a regular octagon. Find ∠m and ∠n.

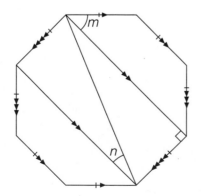

WHOLE NUMBERS

(Practice Problems)

Answer each of the following questions. Show your work and write your statements clearly.

1. Sally's monthly income is $2650. She spends $325 on cosmetics, $760 on clothing, $215 on food, $75 on transport and $415 on other things. If she saves the rest of her income, how much is her total savings for half a year?

2. Andrew estimates that he needs $250 to buy 8 dozen pens and 5 dozen pencils. If each pen costs $3 and each dozen pencils costs $4, find the difference between the actual total cost and the estimated total cost of all the pens and pencils.

3. There are 18 classes of students in a school. 13 of them have 42 students each while the rest have 40 students each. If there are 359 girls in the school, how many boys are there?

4. A man bought 3 tables and 16 chairs. He had estimated that he would need $2500 altogether but that was $129 less than the actual total cost. If each table cost $455, how much did each chair cost?

5. A man bought 18 boxes of 65 apples at $12 per box. He sold 378 of the apples at 3 for $1 and the rest at 4 for $1. Find his total profit.

6. Margaret has two $150 vouchers, five $50 vouchers and six $10 vouchers. Using these, she bought a pair of shoes for $118, a sports bag for $89, a handbag for $365 and two rackets at $75 each. If she paid the outstanding amount in cash, how much did she pay in cash?

7. Julius bought a washing machine with a down payment of $120 and 12 monthly installments of $59. He also bought a refrigerator with a down payment equal to 3 months' installments and $1\frac{1}{2}$ years' monthly installments of $78. How much did he spend on both machines altogether?

8. There were 192 $80 concert tickets, 420 $50 concert tickets and 828 $25 concert tickets for sale. If all the $80 tickets and $50 tickets were sold and the total sale from all the tickets was $56,260, how many $25 tickets were not sold?

9. Red pens are sold in boxes of 18 and blue pens are sold in boxes of 24. Each box of red pens costs $25 while each box of blue pens costs $36. Ryan used $225 to buy some red pens and $504 to buy some blue pens. How many pens did he buy in all?

10. A man has 15 boxes of 8 dozen pens. He repackaged half of the pens into packages of 6 pens and the rest into packages of 9 pens. He sold each package of 6 pens for $3 and each package of 9 pens for $4. Find his total sale.

11. Lionel bought 1 sheet of 50¢ stamps, 4 sheets of 20¢ stamps and 2 sheets of 10¢ stamps. If there were 80 stamps in each sheet and he paid with 3 $50 bills, how much change did he get?

12. Mary has twice as many beads as Lily. Lily has three times as many beads as Tracy. If the three girls have 60 beads altogether, how many more beads does Mary have than Tracy?

Answer each of the following questions. Show your work and write your statements clearly.

13. Mark has three times as many marbles as Bob. Bob has twice as many marbles as Paul. If the three boys have 180 marbles altogether, how many more marbles does Mark have than Paul?

14. Gary has five times as many stickers as Linda. Linda has 15 more stickers than May. If the three students have 230 stickers altogether, how many more stickers does Gary have than May?

15. Lucy and Jean have 240 stickers altogether. If Lucy gives 10 of her stickers to Jean, she will have three times as many stickers as Jean. How many stickers does Lucy have?

16. Peter and Mike have 180 stamps altogether. After Mike gave 20 of his stamps to Peter, he had twice as many stamps as Peter. How many more stamps did Mike have than Peter at first?

17. If Amy gives 10 of her stamps to Robin, she will have four times as many stamps as Robin. If she gives 20 of her stamps to Robin, she will have three times as many stamps as Robin. How many stamps do they have in all?

18. 8 clocks and 5 watches cost $695 altogether. 3 clocks and 3 watches cost $300 altogether. How much more does each clock cost than each watch?

19. There were 476 paper-clips in box A and 52 paper-clips in box B. After an equal number of paper-clips was added into each box, box A had five times as many paper-clips as box B. How many paper-clips were added into box B?

20. An overnight package delivery service charged $16 for every package safely delivered but would pay a penalty of $48 for every package delivered damaged. If it received $9152 for a delivery of 600 packages, how many packages were safely delivered?

21. Peter, Tom and Vincent have 240 cards altogether. Peter gave some of his cards to Tom and the number of Tom's cards was doubled. Then Tom gave some of his cards to Vincent and the number of Vincent's cards was doubled. If the three boys had the same number of cards in the end, how many cards did Peter have at first?

DECIMALS

Answer each of the following questions. Show your work and write your statements clearly.

1. Vincent's monthly income is $1600. He spends 0.05 of it on transport, 0.2 of it on rent, 0.3 of it on food and 0.25 of the rest on others. If he saves the rest of his income, how much money can he save in $\frac{1}{4}$ year?

2. A dressmaker bought 18 yd of cloth at $2.70 per yard and 5 yd of lace at $2.10 per yard. Out of these, she made 6 dresses and sold them at $84.90 each. Find her profit.

3. After giving 10% of her beads to May, 0.15 of them to June and 0.2 of the remainder to March, April had 48 beads left. How many more beads did April give to March than to May?

4.	An hourly rated waiter is paid $2.70 hourly on weekdays and $1.50 more per hour on weekends than on weekdays. If he works from 9 a.m. to 10 p.m. on weekdays and from 10 a.m. to 5 p.m. on weekends, find his weekly income.

5.	The total cost of 23 binders, 7 notebooks and 15 staplers is $177. If each binder costs $4.90 and each stapler costs $2.70, find the cost of each notebook.

6.	Albert had 16.2 l of gas in his car tank when he started on his journey. After travelling for some time, he had only 3.6 l of gas left and he refilled $30 worth of gas at $1 per liter. At the end of his journey, his gas level was 2.8 l. If he travelled 1 km with every 0.2 l of gas, find the total distance he covered.

7. Each gallon of milk cost cost $1.20 more than each bottle of drink. Amy bought 9 gallons of milk for $21.60. Alice bought 4 gallons of milk and 5 bottles of drink. How much less money did Alice spend than Amy?

8. Wendy bought 4 slacks, 3 shirts and 2 skirts for $167.90 altogether. She paid $16.50 for each shirt and $21.40 for each skirt. If she had bought 3 slacks, 2 shirts and 4 skirts instead, how much more money must she pay?

9. Mike bought some books and magazines for $122.60 altogether. Each book cost $14.90 and each magazine cost $6.10. If he bought 4 more books than magazines, how many books and magazines did he buy in all?

10. 0.2 of Hazel's paper-clips are red, $\frac{1}{5}$ of them are blue, 0.3 of them are yellow and 0.4 of the rest are green. If she has 4 more red paper-clips than green paper-clips, how many paper-clips does she have?

11. James has 0.4 times as many stamps as Dave and 0.5 times as many stamps as Joe. If the 3 boys have 330 stamps altogether, how many more stamps does Dave have than Joe?

12. 0.5 of Jason's stickers is equal to 0.2 of William's stickers. If they have 70 stickers altogether, how many stickers does Jason have?

Answer each of the following questions. Show your work and write your statements clearly.

13. Rose has 0.25 times as many stickers as Fion and Fion has 0.8 times as many stickers as Pam. If the three girls have 480 stickers altogether, how many more stickers does Pam have than Rose after Pam gives 0.2 of her stickers away?

14. Rick has 1.75 times as many marbles as Karl. Rick bought another 10 marbles, and now has twice as many marbles as Karl. How many marbles do they have altogether now?

15. Each pencil cost $0.30 less than each ruler and each ruler cost $0.40 less than each pen. Weimin bought 2 pencils, 2 rulers and 5 pens and paid $5.45 altogether. How much did each ruler cost?

16. 7 spoons and 8 forks cost $12.80 altogether. 4 spoons and 5 forks cost $5.10 less. How much more does each fork cost than each spoon?

17. Vivian bought some apples and oranges for $16.95 altogether. Each apple cost $0.45 and each orange cost $0.10 more than each apple. If she bought 9 more oranges than apples, how many apples did she buy?

18. Andrew and Joseph have some money each. If Andrew gives $4.80 to Joseph, they will each have an equal amount of money. If Joseph gives $4.80 to Andrew, Andrew will have three times as much money as Joseph. How much money do they have altogether?

19. Jolene had $75.20 more than Cindy. After Jolene gave $3.60 to Cindy, she had five times as much money as Cindy. How much money did Jolene have at first?

20. A library imposes a fine of $0.20 per day for each book returned late and a renewal fee of $0.60 for each book renewed. On a certain day, there were twice as many late returns of books as book renewals, and the total sum of money collected from the fines and renewals was $346. If all the books returned late were each one day overdue, how much more money was collected from the book renewals than the late returns of books?

21. A transport company charged $5.50 for each item safely delivered but paid $14.50 for each item delivered damaged and $51.50 for each item lost. It collected $627 for a delivery of 170 items, out of which 4 items were delivered damaged. How many items were lost?

REVIEW PROBLEMS 3

AREA AND PERIMETER

Practice Problems

Answer each of the following questions. Show your work and write your statements clearly.

1. A rectangular farm 74 yd wide has an area of 11,692 yd². Find the cost of fencing it at $12 per yard.

2. In the figure shown, find its area and perimeter. (Take π = 3.14)

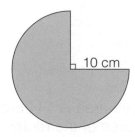

10 cm

3. The figure shows a square ABCD. AD is the diameter of the semi-circle. Find the shaded area. $\left(\text{Take } \pi = \frac{22}{7}\right)$

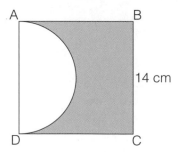

14 cm

4. Lionel pasted a rectangular photograph onto a rectangular piece of cardboard as shown. Find the area of the cardboard not covered by the photograph.

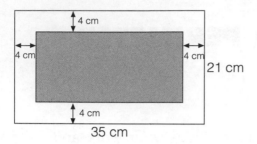

5. It costs $92,708 to till a rectangular farm 86 m wide at $7 per square meter. How much less does it cost to fence it at $15 per meter than to till it?

6. A rectangle is three times as long as a square whose area is 144 cm^2. If the rectangle is half as wide as it is long, find the area of the rectangle.

7. The ratio of the length of a rectangle to its width is 5 : 2. If its perimeter is 56 cm and a square 5 cm long is cut away from the rectangle, what is the area of the rectangle left?

8. In the figure shown, find the perimeter. (Take π = 3.14)

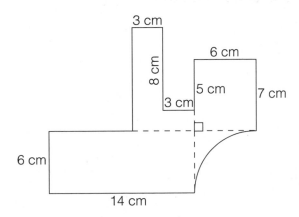

3 cm

8 cm

6 cm

5 cm

3 cm

7 cm

6 cm

14 cm

9. A square and a rectangle have the same area. The rectangle is 25 cm long and has a perimeter of 68 cm. Find the length of the square.

10. A circle and a rectangle have the same area. The circle has a diameter of 42 cm and the rectangle has a width of 18 cm. Find the perimeter of the rectangle. $\left(\text{Take } \pi = \frac{22}{7} \right)$

11. In the figure shown, what is the shaded area?

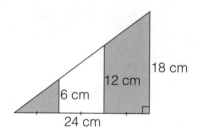

12. The figure shows a garden with a circular pond in it. Find the cost of covering the garden with grass at $24 per square feet. (Take $\pi = 3.14$)

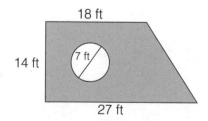

Answer each of the following questions. Show your work and write your statements clearly.

13. In the figure shown, ABCDE is the arc of a semi-circle whose diameter is 56 cm. AGC and CFE are the arcs of two identical quadrants. What is the area of the shaded parts? $\left(\text{Take } \pi = \dfrac{22}{7}\right)$

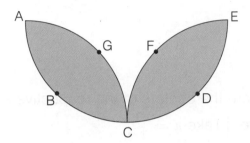

14. In the figure shown, PQRS is a square with sides 35 cm long. PSTQ is a quadrant. What is the shaded area? $\left(\text{Take } \pi = \dfrac{22}{7}\right)$

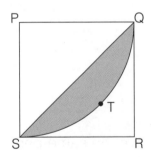

15. In the figure shown, WXYZ is a rectangle. Find the area of the shaded part.

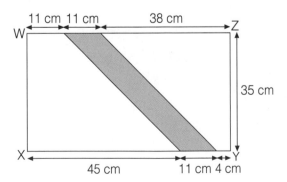

16. In the figure shown, ABC is a right-angled triangle and ADB and BDC are semi-circles of radii 18 cm. Find the area of the shaded parts. (Take π = 3.14)

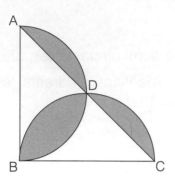

17. In the figure shown, A, B and C are the centers of the respective semi-circles. Find the area of the figure. $\left(\text{Take } \pi = \frac{22}{7} \right)$

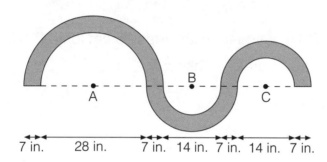

7 in.　　28 in.　　7 in.　14 in.　7 in.　14 in.　7 in.

18. In the figure shown, the circle and the square have the same perimeter. Find the difference in their areas. $\left(\text{Take } \pi = \frac{22}{7} \right)$

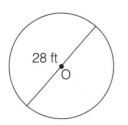

28 ft

O

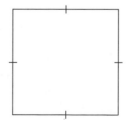

19. In the figure shown, BH // CG and DF is the diameter of the semi-circle. AE = 37.8 cm, BH = DF = 30 cm and CD = FG = 10 cm. Find the shaded area. (Take π = 3.14)

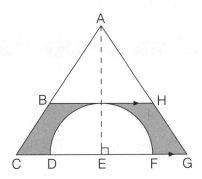

20. The figure shown is made up of 4 different quadrants. Find its perimeter. $\left(\text{Take } \pi = \dfrac{22}{7} \right)$

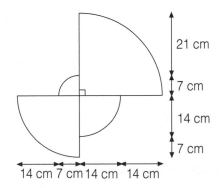

21 cm
7 cm
14 cm
7 cm

14 cm 7 cm 14 cm 14 cm

21. In the figure shown, O is the center of the circle whose radius is 20 in. OABC is a square and OPQ is a right-angled triangle. OP = OQ = 36 in. Find the area of the figure. (Take π = 3.14)

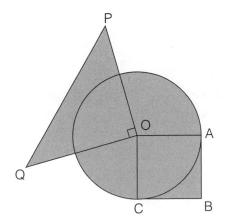

BAR GRAPHS AND LINE GRAPHS

Study each graph carefully and then answer the questions that follow.

1. The bar graph shows the total number of tickets sold for a concert that was held on 3 different days.

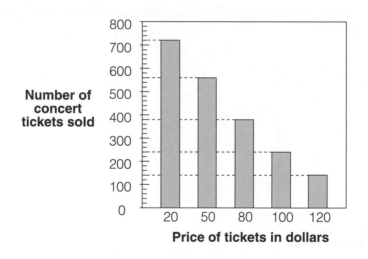

Number of concert tickets sold

Price of tickets in dollars

a. If the seating capacity for the concert was 800 persons per day, find the average number of seats that were unoccupied on the 3 days.

b. What was the total amount of money collected from the sale of tickets that were priced at $20, $50 and $100 each?

2. The bar graph shows the number of people who are fans of 6 different TV stars.

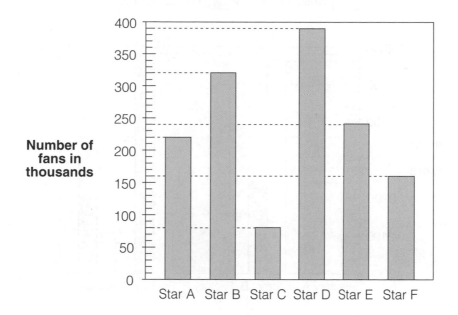

a. Express the number of fans star E has as a percentage of the total number of fans stars E and F have.

b. If star B has 112,000 male fans, what is the ratio of the number of her male fans to the number of her female fans?

c. Calculate the average number of fans stars A, B, C, D and E have.

3. The bar graph shows the number of workers in 5 different factories.

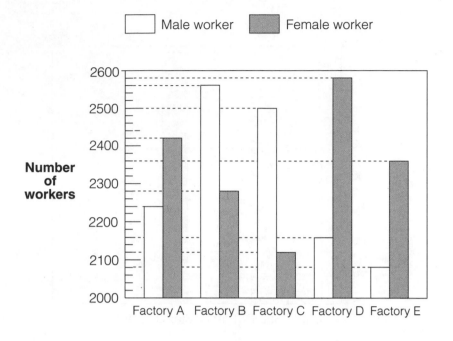

a. What is the ratio of the number of male workers in factory A to the number of male workers in factory D to the number of male workers in factory E?

b. Find the average number of workers in factories A, B, C and D.

c. 560 workers from factory B were transferred to factory E and another 850 workers from factory B were transferred to factory C. Find the total number of workers left in factories B and C.

4. The bar graph shows the number of television viewers who voted on whether they liked or disliked 5 different television commercials.

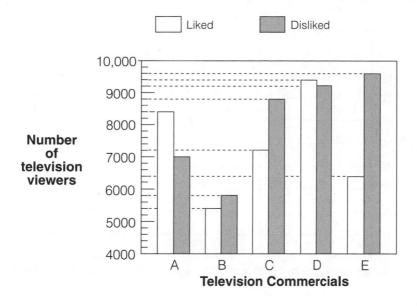

a. Which commercial has the highest percentage of viewers who disliked it? How many per cent of viewers disliked it?

b. Which commercial attracted the most number of votes? How many votes did it attract?

c. 930 of the viewers who voted on commercial B also voted on commercial A and 1790 of the viewers who voted on commerical A also voted on commercial B. Find the total number of actual viewers who voted on commercials A and B.

5. The line graph shows the journeys of a car and a truck between town A and town B that were 100 km apart.

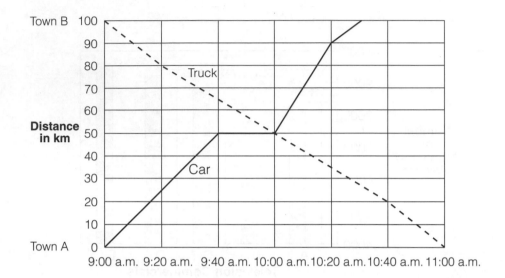

a. How far away from town A was the truck when it passed the car?

b. How far apart were the car and the truck at 9:20 a.m.?

c. Find the average speed of the truck for the whole journey.

6. The line graph shows the number of people who died from cancer and heart diseases between 1989 and 1998 in a certain country.

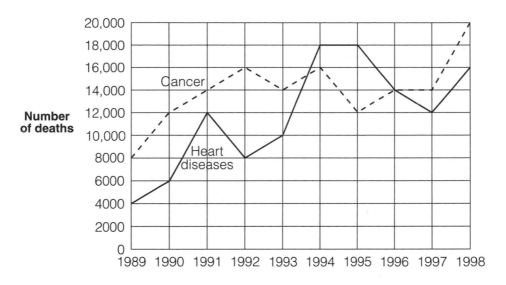

a. How many more people died from cancer than heart diseases from 1991 to 1994?

b. Express the total number of people who died from heart diseases as a fraction of the total number of people who died from cancer from 1989 to 1990.

c. In which year was the difference between the number of deaths due to cancer and that due to heart diseases the greatest? What was the difference?

7. The line graph shows the number of new subscribers for Magazine A and Magazine B between January and October last year.

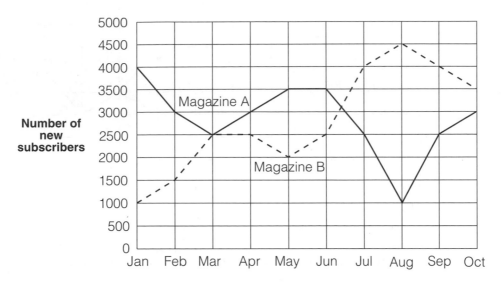

a. How many more new subscribers did Magazine A attract than Magazine B between January and June?

b. Find the average number of new subscribers Magazine B attracted monthly between June and October.

c. What was the largest percentage decrease from one month to the next in the number of new subscribers for Magazine A?

8. The line graph shows the monthly incomes of Mr. Albert, Mr. Patrick and Mr. Damien last year.

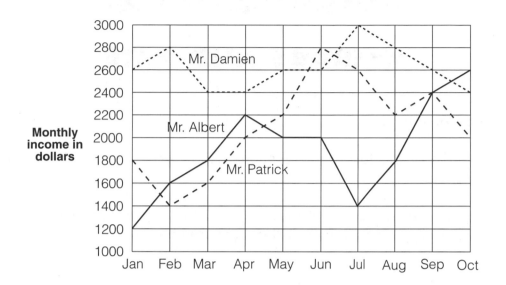

a. In which month was the difference between Mr. Patrick's income and Mr. Damien's income the greatest? How much was the difference?

b. What was the average monthly income of the three men between January and March? Give your answer correct to the nearest dollar.

c. If Mr. Albert spent 65% of his October income and Mr. Patrick spent 45% of his October income, how much more money did Mr. Patrick save than Mr. Albert in October?

AVERAGE AND RATE

Practice Problems

Answer each of the following questions. Show your work and write your statements clearly.

1. 3 boys have an average of $1.60. 4 girls have an average of $2.30. What is the average sum of money the 7 children have?

2. Jane and Wendy weigh 94.6 kg altogether. Jane and May have an average weight of 48.3 kg. If Wendy weighs 2.4 kg more than Jane, find the average weight of Wendy and May.

3. Lina bought 2 dresses at $41.50 each and a shirt for $7.90. Macy bought 3 dresses at $89.90 each and 3 skirts at $47 each. Altogether, how much did each of them spend on the average?

4. Sandra's monthly income for a year was $2180. For the first 4 months of the year, she spent an average of $1580 per month. For the remaining 8 months, she spent an average of $1760. Find her average monthly savings.

5. The average cost of 4 books and 2 magazines is $6.10. The average cost of 2 books and 1 dictionary is $10.40. If the average cost of the 4 books is $6.90, find the average cost of 1 magazine and 1 dictionary.

6. 6 girls have an average of 18 stickers. When 3 more girls join in, the 9 girls have an average of 27 stickers. If a tenth girl has 25 stickers, what is the average number of stickers the 3 new girls and the tenth girl have?

7. A taxi charged $2.20 for the first 2 mi travelled and $0.10 for each additional half-mile or part thereof. Janet took a taxi from her house to the airport, which was 23.4 mi away. If she paid the driver $20, how much change did she get?

8. A book distributor charges $19.90 for the first book ordered through a book order. It charges $17.50 for each of the next 4 books and $16.90 for every subsequent book thereafter. How much must Peter pay if he were to order 10 books through this book order?

9. The table below shows the rates of pay of a waiter on weekdays (Mondays to Fridays).

Time	Hourly Pay
9 a.m. – 12 p.m.	$2.40
12 p.m. – 2 p.m.	$3.10
2 p.m. – 7 p.m.	$2.70
7 p.m. – 9 p.m.	$3.50

If he works from 9 a.m. to 9 p.m. on every weekday, find his total weekly income.

10. The table below shows the admission charges to an adult recreational club.

	Member	Non-member
Male	$27	$35
Female	$24	$30

A group of friends, made up of 4 male members, 1 female member, 2 male non-members and 3 female non-members, visited the club. How much did they pay for their admission altogether?

11. The table below shows the selling prices of greeting cards.

Number of Sets	Selling Price
1 – 5	$9.80 per set
6 – 15	$9.50 per set
16 – 25	$9.10 per set
> 26	$8.80 per set

Sally bought 3 sets of greeting cards, Steven bought 9 sets and Mary bought 15 sets. How much money could they have saved altogether if they had bought the greeting cards together?

12. It cost $12 to send a type A package and $18 to send a type B package. Albert sent some type A and type B packages and paid $612 altogether. If he sent 9 type A packages, how many type B packages did he send?

Challenging Problems

Answer each of the following questions. Show your work and write your statements clearly.

13. For each of the first 200 units of a calculator a salesman sells, he gets a commission of $0.80. For each of the next 200 units he sells, he gets a commission of $0.90. For each subsequent unit he sells thereafter, he gets a commission of $1. How many units must he sell to earn a total commission of $420?

14. The table below shows the rates of charge for household water usage.

For the first 75 units	$0.20 per unit
For the next 100 units	$0.30 per unit
For the next 125 units thereafter	$0.40 per unit
For all units thereafter	$0.50 per unit

If a certain household has to pay $110 for water usage this month, how many units of water has it used?

15. The table below shows the annual rates of interest paid on a bank's fixed deposits.

For the first $50,000	4%
For the next $50,000	3%
For the next $100,000	2%
For any additional amount exceeding $200,000	1%

A man had a fixed deposit account in the bank. If he received $6000 interest last year, what was his principal sum in his fixed deposit account?

GENERAL REVIEW

(Practice Problems)

Answer each of the following questions. Show your work and write your statements clearly.

1. Mark has 200 marbles. $\frac{1}{8}$ of them are blue, $\frac{3}{20}$ of them are red, $\frac{1}{5}$ of them are green and $\frac{1}{3}$ of the remainder are yellow. How many yellow marbles does he have?

2. Lishan gave $\frac{1}{4}$ of her beads to Joey, $\frac{3}{16}$ of her beads to May and $\frac{1}{5}$ of the rest of her beads to Aminah. If she had 36 beads left, how many beads did she have at first?

3. The number of Jason's cards and the number of Frederick's cards are in the ratio 5 : 8. The number of Frederick's cards and the number of Steven's cards are in the ratio 4 : 3. If Jason has 18 fewer cards than Frederick, how many cards does Steven have?

4. The number of Paul's paper-clips and the number of Andy's paper-clips were in the ratio 4 : 5. After Paul used 25% of his paper-clips and Andy used 60% of his paper-clips, they had 60 paper-clips left altogether. How many more paper-clips did Andy have than Paul at first?

5. Jane and Lisa have 180 beads altogether. 40% of the beads are Jane's and the rest are Lisa's. 50% of Jane's beads and 25% of Lisa's beads are red. How many more red beads does Jane have than Lisa?

6. Steven sold two computers at $3200 each. He made a profit of 25% on one computer but a loss of 20% on the other computer. Find his total net profit or loss.

7. A truck travelled at an average speed of 54 mi/h on a 135-mi journey. For the first part of the journey, it travelled at an average speed of 40 mi/h for $\frac{3}{4}$ h. Calculate its average speed for the rest of the journey.

8. Raymond and Mark set off from the same place at 7:40 a.m. and travelled along a straight road. Raymond travelled at a uniform speed of 90 km/h while Mark travelled at a uniform speed of 80 km/h. After travelling 360 km, Raymond stopped to take a rest. When Mark caught up with Raymond, they both set off together again.
   (a) At what time did Mark catch up with Raymond?
   (b) How long was Raymond's rest?

9. The figure shows a square 28 cm long with 4 equal quadrants inscribed within. Find the area and perimeter of the shaded part. $\left(\text{Take } \pi = \frac{22}{7} \right)$

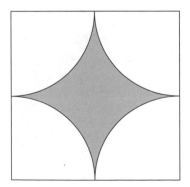

10. Find the area and perimeter of the figure shown. (Take π = 3.14)

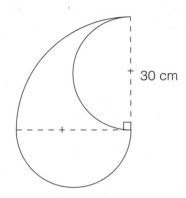

30 cm

11. There are 4a marbles in each bag and 3a^2 marbles in each box. There are 2a bags and 4a boxes.
    (a) How many marbles are there altogether? Give your answer in terms of a.
    (b) If a = 12, how many marbles are there altogether?

12. A jug of 2x l of drink is poured into 7 glasses and 10x cups. Each glass has a capacity of 0.2 l.
    (a) Find the capacity of each cup, leaving your answer in terms of x.
    (b) If x = 2, find the capacity of x cups.

13. The total volume of water and 8 identical beads in a beaker is 1194 cm³. When 3 of the beads are removed, the total volume of the water and beads decreases to 990 cm³. Find the volume of the water in the beaker.

14. Five 5-cm metal cubes and thirteen 2-cm metal cubes were melted and recast into a new metal cube. Find the length of the new metal cube.

15. In the figure shown, not drawn to scale, AB // CD. Find ∠y.

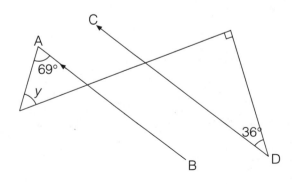

16. In the figure shown, not drawn to scale, O is the center of the smaller circle. Find $\angle x$ and $\angle y$.

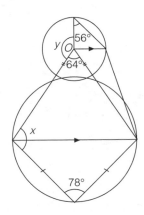

17. A shopkeeper bought 9 boxes of 84 oranges at $17 per box. He sold 300 oranges at 4 for $1 and the remaining oranges at 3 for $1. What was his total profit?

18. Darren has 0.75 times as many action figures as Lionel. Lionel has 4 times as many action figures as Paul. If Darren has 24 action figures more than Paul, how many action figures do the three boys have altogether?

19. The total height of Jim and Irene is 2.98 m. The total height of Irene and Mark is 2.94 m. If Mark is 0.02 m taller than Irene, how much taller is Jim than Mark?

20. The average cost of 6 binders is $3.80. The average cost of another 2 binders is $4.40. What is the average cost of all the binders?

21. A metal spring will extend proportionally with every 50 g of weight when it is stretched. When the spring is stretched by a weight of 150 g, its net reading is 23 cm. When the spring is stretched by a weight of 250 g, its net reading is 24 cm. Find the actual length of the spring when it is not stretched.

22. For every 25 stamps that Jane has, Mike has 40 stamps. If Mike has 90 stamps more than Jane, how many stamps do they have in all?

23. For every $100 that Vivian spends, $38 is spent on clothing, $25 is spent on cosmetics, $20 is spent on hair styling and the rest is spent on other things. If she spends a total of $850, how much more money does she spend on clothing than on cosmetics?

24. Amy bought 8 notebooks for $3.60 and 6 plastic book covers for $3. If she had bought a dozen notebooks and 9 plastic book covers, how much more money must she pay?

Answer each of the following questions. Show your work and write your statements clearly.

25. Sam has $\frac{7}{10}$ as many marbles as Lionel. Lionel has $\frac{1}{2}$ as many marbles as Ian. If the three boys have 148 marbles altogether, how many marbles does Sam have?

26. $\frac{1}{4}$ of Pamela's coins is equal to $\frac{1}{5}$ of Michael's coins. If Pamela has 20 coins fewer than Michael, how many coins will Michael have if Pamela gives $\frac{1}{2}$ of her coins to him?

27. If Lisa gives away $\frac{1}{5}$ of her beads and Alice gives away 10 of her beads, Lisa will have $\frac{1}{2}$ as many beads as Alice. How many more beads does Alice have than Lisa if they have 140 beads altogether?

28. The ratio of John's money to Eric's money was 7 : 2. After John spent $26 and Eric saved another $14, they each had the same amount of money. How much money did John and Eric have altogether at first?

29. The ratio of the number of apples to the number of pears in a basket was 6 : 5. After 16 apples and pears were added into the basket, the ratio of the number of apples to the number of pears became 9 : 8. If there were 80 pears in the basket in the end, how many apples were added into the basket?

30. A man deposited $30,000 in a bank that paid an annual simple interest of 2%. He withdrew $5000 from the bank 6 months later and put this money into another bank that paid an annual simple interest rate of 3%. Find the total amount of money he had in both banks 12 months after his initial deposit.

31. Cindy had four times as many postcards as Annie. After Cindy gave 20% of her postcards to Jane and Annie gave 10% of her postcards to Jane, the number of Jane's postcards increased by 75%. If Jane had 252 postcards in the end, how many postcards did Cindy have at first?

32. Bob and Perry set off from town A to town B, at uniform speeds of 84 km/h and 96 km/h respectively, at the same time. After some time, they were 42 km apart. How long had they been travelling?

33. Towns M and N were 600 km apart. At 6:20 p.m., Ken set off from town M to town N at a constant speed of 80 km/h while Jim set off from town N to town M at a constant speed of 120 km/h.
    (a) At what time did they meet on the road?
    (b) How far away was Jim from town M when he met Ken?

34. The figure shows a container. If water is poured into it up to a depth of 13 cm, how much more water can it hold?

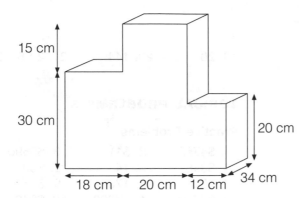

35. Jennifer has 18 more buttons than Lucy. Angie has three times as many buttons as Jennifer. The three girls have 252 buttons in all. How many buttons does Angie have?

36. If Peter gives 32 stamps to William, he will have four times as many stamps as William. If he gives 20 stamps to William, he will have five times as many stamps as William. How many stamps does Peter have?

ANSWERS

TOPICAL PROBLEMS 1

Practice Problems

1. (a) $100 - 4k$ (b) 64
2. (a) $18 + 18x$ (b) 72
3. (a) $\dfrac{90 + m}{2}$ (b) 55
4. (a) $\$(7a + 14)$ (b) \$119
5. (a) $\$\dfrac{50 - p}{8}$ (b) \$4
6. (a) $\$8y$ (b) \$16
7. (a) $\$(12z + 8)$ (b) \$176
8. (a) $\$\dfrac{3q}{4}$ (b) \$30
9. (a) \$1320   (b) \$1375
10. (a) $\$19a$ (b) \$76
11. (a) $13b$ (b) 351
12. (a) $\$\dfrac{4c}{3}$ (b) \$1

Challenging Problems

13. (a) 20   (b) 40
14. (a) $20s - 28$ (b) 132
15. (a) $\dfrac{3w + 9w^2}{3}$ (b) 114
16. (a) $124x$ cm   (b) 620 cm
17. (a) $\$18p^3$ (b) \$144
18. (a) $\$18q$ (b) 288
19. (a) $\$6x$ (b) \$72
20. (a) $\$(4p - 6)$ (b) \$14
21. (a) $30k^2(2k - 7)$ cm^2
     (b) 281,880 cm^2

TOPICAL PROBLEMS 2

Practice Problems

1. 20   2. 4   3. 240
4. 40   5. \$18   6. \$600
7. 15   8. 35   9. \$6
10. 24   11. 42   12. \$50

Challenging Problems

13. \$4   14. 54   15. 88
16. 9   17. 1 : 9   18. 9 years

19. 20   20. 144   21. 2 : 8 : 3

TOPICAL PROBLEMS 3

Practice Problems

1. \$4752   2. \$11   3. \$9590
4. \$348   5. 14   6. 360
7. 120   8. 170   9. 54
10. \$2700   11. \$7200   12. \$840

Challenging Problems

13. 40%   14. \$2500   15. \$4000
16. \$2000   17. \$2000   18. \$600
19. 195   20. 306   21. 100

TOPICAL PROBLEMS 4

Practice Problems

1. 100 km/h   2. $78\frac{2}{5}$ km/h   3. 411 km
4. 6.50 p.m.   5. $\frac{1}{2}$ h   6. 50 mi/h
7. 75 km   8. $259\frac{1}{5}$ km   9. $\frac{5}{8}$ h
10. 315 km   11. 60 km/h   12. 186 km

Challenging Problems

13. $1\frac{2}{3}$ h   14. 112 km/h   15. 105 km/h
16. 10 km   17. 11:45 a.m.
18. $12\frac{1}{2}$ km
19. (a) 6:20 p.m.   (b) 9:20 p.m.
20. (a) 7:03 a.m.   (b) 162 km
21. (a) 80 km/h   (b) $\frac{5}{8}$ h

TOPICAL PROBLEM 5

Practice Problems

1. 24   2. \$21.60   3. 4
4. 180   5. \$50   6. 28

7. $360   8. 46   9. $30
10. $5   11. $26   12. 19

Challenging Problems

13. 60   14. 20   15. 50
16. 50   17. 5   18. 60
19. 162   20. $11   21. 200

TOPICAL PROBLEMS 6

Practice Problems

1. 160 cm   2. 3384 yd   3. 81.64 cm
4. 942 cm^2 5. 2612.48 cm^2
6. 427.9 cm^2 7. 329.7 cm^2
8. 69 cm   9. 56.52 m
10. 32.13 cm   11. 87.24 cm^2
12. 1232 cm^2, 176 cm

Challenging Problems

13. 247.06 in^2 14. 700 cm^2
15. 119.652 cm^2 16. 189 cm^2
17. 1008 cm^2 18. 172 cm^2
19. 1271.7 cm^2 20. 306.6 cm
21. 5292 cm^2

TOPICAL PROBLEMS 7

Practice Problems

1. 30 min   2. 24 cm   3. 1.5 cm
4. 3 cm   5. 11.5 cm   6. 3000 cm^3
7. 3281.25 cm^3 8. 11,875 cm^3
9. 324 cm^3 10. 9 cm
11. 60 cm^3 12. 2 cm

Challenging Problems

13. 1968 cm^3 14. 10,008 cm^2
15. 2.75 m   16. 15,606 cm^3
17. 2360 cm^3 18. 10 h
19. 1050 cm^3 20. 3.52 cm
21. 44,220 g

TOPICAL PROBLEMS 8

Practice Problems

1. 52°   2. 80°   3. 100°
4. 33°   5. 80°   6. 106°, 37°
7. 146°   8. 80°   9. 113°
10. 74°   11. 53°   12. 40°, 50°

Challenging Problems

13. 50°   14. 13°   15. 98°, 37°
16. 24°, 102°   17. 80°, 100°   18. 108°, 140°
19. 28°   20. 76°   21. 45°, 22.5°

REVIEW PROBLEMS 1

Practice Problems

1. $5160   2. $58   3. 387
4. $79   5. $108   6. $112
7. $2466   8. 32   9. 498
10. $680   11. $30   12. 30

Challenging Problems

13. 100   14. 155   15. 190
16. 100   17. 200   18. $30
19. 54   20. 593   21. 140

REVIEW PROBLEMS 2

Practice Problems

1. $1620   2. $450.30   3. 4
4. $234.30   5. $3.40   6. 217 km
7. $6   8. $7.40   9. 10
10. 50   11. 30   12. 20

Challenging Problems

13. 144   14. 120   15. $0.45
16. $0.10   17. 12   18. $38.40
19. $88.60   20. $69.20   21. 4

REVIEW PROBLEM 3

Practice Problems

1. $5568   2. $235.5 cm^2, 67.1 cm
3. 119 cm^2 4. 384 cm^2 5. $85,508
6. 648 cm^2 7. 135 cm^2 8. 79.42 cm
9. 15 cm   10. 190 cm   11. 144 cm^2
12. $6636.84

Challenging Problems

13. 896 cm^2 14. 350 cm^2 15. 385 cm^2
16. 369.36 cm^2 17. 847 $in.^2$
18. 132 ft^2 19. 254.75 cm^2
20. 166 cm   21. 1676 $in.^2$

REVIEW PROBLEMS 4

Practice Problems

1. (a) 120   (b) $66,400
2. (a) 60%   (b) 7 : 13
   (c) 250,000
3. (a) 28 : 27 : 26 (b) 4740
   (c) 8900
4. (a) Commercial E, 60%
   (b) Commercial D, 18,600
   (c) 23,880
5. (a) 50 km   (b) 55 km
   (c) 50 km/h
6. (a) 12,000   (b) $\frac{1}{2}$
   (c) 1992, 8000
7. (a) 7500   (b) 3700
   (c) 60%
8. (a) February, $1400
   (b) $1911   (c) $190

REVIEW PROBLEM 5

Practice Problems

1. $2   2. 49.5 kg   3. $250.80
4. $480   5. $10.95   6. 40
7. $13.50   8. $174.40   9. $169.50
10. $292   11. $19.80   12. 28

Challenging Problems

13. 480   14. 330   15. $250,000

REVIEW PROBLEMS 6

Practice Problems

1. 35   2. 80   3. 36
4. 12   5. 9
6. Loss, $160   7. 60 mi/h
8. (a) 12:10 p.m.   (b) $\frac{1}{2}$ h
9. 168 cm^2, 88 cm
10. 706.5 cm^2, 141.3 cm
11. (a) $8a^2 + 12a^3$ (b) 21,888
12. (a) $\frac{2x - 1.4}{10x}$ l (b) 0.26 l
13. 650 cm^3 14. 9 cm
15. 57°   16. 109°, 170°
17. $74   18. 96
19. 0.04 m   20. $3.95
21. 21.5 cm   22. 390
23. $110.50   24. $3.30

Challenging Problems

25. 28   26. 140   27. 40
28. $72   29. 6   30. $30,625
31. 480   32. $3\frac{1}{2}$ h
33. (a) 9:20 p.m.   (b) 240 km
34. 35,020 cm^3 35. 162
36. 320